The B2B Content Marketing Handbook

How B2B Organizations Can Win with Content Marketing Today

Emmanuel O. Egaga

Copyright

All rights reserved. No part of this publication may be reproduced, distributed, or transmitted in any form or by any means, including photocopying, recording, or other electronic or mechanical methods, without the prior written permission of the publisher, except in the case of brief quotations embodied in critical reviews and certain other noncommercial uses permitted by copyright law.

Copyright © 2024 by Emmanuel O Egaga

Disclaimer:

The information provided in this book is for educational and informational purposes only. While every effort has been made to ensure the accuracy and completeness of the content, the author and publisher make no representations or warranties of any kind, express or implied, about the absolute suitability, reliability, or availability of the information contained herein. Any reliance you place on such information is therefore strictly at your own risk.

In no event shall the author or publisher be liable for any damages including, but not limited to, indirect or consequential damages, or any damages whatsoever arising from the use or performance of this book.

About the Book

"Success in B2B content marketing is a journey, not a destination."

Are you ready to revolutionize your B2B marketing strategies and achieve unparalleled success? Look no further than The B2B Content Marketing Handbook: How B2B Organizations Can Win with Content Marketing.

In this comprehensive guide, you'll embark on a transformative journey that will empower you to:

1. Master Content Creation: Learn the art of crafting compelling content that captivates your audience, drives engagement, and fosters lasting relationships.

2. Drive Customer Engagement: Discover proven strategies to connect with your target audience on a deeper level, leveraging data-driven insights to deliver personalized experiences that resonate.

3. Establish Thought Leadership: Position your brand as an industry authority, cultivate trust, and influence purchasing decisions with thought-provoking content that showcases your expertise.

4. Optimize Performance: Gain actionable techniques to measure, analyze, and optimize your content performance, ensuring maximum impact and ROI.

5. Stay Ahead of Trends: Stay ahead of the curve with insights into emerging trends, innovative technologies, and best practices that will keep your B2B content marketing strategies ahead of the competition.

Benefits of The B2B Content Marketing Handbook:

1. Practical Strategies: Access actionable tips, strategies, and frameworks that you can implement immediately to elevate your content marketing efforts.

2. Real-World Examples: Dive into case studies and success stories from leading B2B organizations, gaining valuable insights and inspiration for your own campaigns.
3. Expert Guidance: Benefit from the expertise of seasoned marketing professionals, thought leaders, and industry experts who share their insights and best practices.
4. Emotionally Engaging: Experience a journey that goes beyond tactics and metrics, delving into the emotional impact of storytelling, connection-building, and brand loyalty.

Are you ready to unleash the full potential of B2B content marketing and propel your business to new heights? Get your copy of **The B2B Content Marketing Handbook** today and embark on a transformative path to success!

About the Author

Emmanuel O. Egaga is a visionary marketer, content strategist, and thought leader in the world of content marketing. With over a decade of experience driving impactful marketing campaigns for leading organizations, Emmanuel has honed his expertise in crafting compelling narratives that resonate with audiences and drive measurable results.

Throughout his career, Emmanuel has been passionate about empowering businesses to harness the power of content to connect, engage, and inspire action. His innovative approach to content marketing has helped numerous B2B organizations achieve unprecedented success in today's competitive landscape.

Emmanuel's dedication to excellence and commitment to continuous learning have earned him recognition as a trusted advisor and strategic partner for businesses seeking to elevate their marketing strategies. He believes in the transformative power of storytelling, data-driven insights, and personalized experiences to drive meaningful connections and foster brand loyalty.

In **The B2B Content Marketing Handbook**, Emmanuel shares his wealth of knowledge, practical strategies, and actionable insights to guide you on a journey of success in B2B content marketing. Through real-world examples, case studies, and expert advice, Emmanuel equips you with the tools and techniques you need to thrive in the ever-evolving digital landscape.

Join Emmanuel on a transformative journey as he demystifies the complexities of B2B content marketing and empowers you to unlock the full potential of your marketing efforts. Get ready to inspire, engage, and win with content marketing like never before!

Connect with him via LinkedIn on: www.linkedin.com/in/emmanuelegaga

Introduction

Welcome to The B2B Content Marketing Handbook: How B2B Organizations Can Win with Content Marketing!

In today's dynamic business landscape, content marketing has emerged as the cornerstone of success for B2B organizations. It's not just about selling products or services; it's about crafting compelling narratives, building meaningful connections, and inspiring action.

This handbook is your roadmap to navigating the complexities of B2B content marketing with confidence and finesse. Whether you're a seasoned marketing professional or embarking on your content journey, this book is designed to equip you with practical strategies, actionable insights, and real-world examples that will propel your B2B marketing efforts to new heights.

Discover how to:

- Create captivating content that resonates with your target audience
- Leverage data-driven strategies for personalized customer experiences
- Cultivate thought leadership and establish industry authority
- Harness the power of storytelling to drive engagement and conversions

- Measure and optimize content performance for maximum impact

Join us on this transformative journey as we unlock the secrets to winning with content marketing in the competitive B2B landscape. Get ready to inspire, connect, and thrive with The B2B Content Marketing Handbook!

Table of Content

Copyright
About The Book
About The Author
Introduction

1. Introduction to B2B Content Marketing
   - Definition and Importance of B2B Content Marketing
   - Key Differences Between B2B and B2C Content Marketing
   - Evolution and Trends in B2B Content Marketing
2. Understanding B2B Buyer Personas
   - Importance of Buyer Personas in B2B Marketing
   - How to Create Effective B2B Buyer Personas

- Utilizing Buyer Personas for Targeted Content Creation
3. Content Strategy Development
   - Building a Comprehensive B2B Content Strategy
   - Aligning Content Strategy with Business Goals
   - Content Mapping for Various Stages of the Buyer's Journey
4. Creating Compelling B2B Content
   - Types of Content That Work Best in B2B Marketing (e.g., whitepapers, case studies, webinars)
   - Crafting Engaging and Valuable Content for B2B Audiences

- Incorporating Data and Insights into Content Creation
5. Optimizing Content for Search Engines and Social Media
    - SEO Strategies for B2B Content Marketing
    - Leveraging Social Media Platforms for B2B Content Distribution
    - Best Practices for Content Amplification and Promotion
6. Measuring and Analyzing B2B Content Marketing Success
    - Key Metrics and KPIs for B2B Content Performance
    - Tools and Techniques for Content Performance Tracking

- Interpreting Data to Improve Content Marketing ROI
7. Personalization and Account-Based Marketing (ABM)
    - Importance of Personalization in B2B Content Marketing
    - Implementing Account-Based Marketing Strategies
    - Tailoring Content for Target Accounts and Decision Makers
8. Building Strong Relationships Through Content
    - Nurturing Leads with Content Marketing Automation

- Creating Content for Customer Retention and Upselling
- Strategies for Building Trust and Authority in B2B Markets

9. Content Collaboration and Partnerships
    - Collaborating with Industry Influencers and Thought Leaders
    - Partnering with Complementary Businesses for Co-Marketing Opportunities
    - Leveraging Content Syndication and Guest Posting

10. Adapting to Emerging Trends in B2B Content Marketing
    - AI and Machine Learning in Content Personalization
    - Interactive Content Strategies for B2B Engagement
    - Future Outlook and Predictions for B2B Content Marketing

28

Chapter 1: Introduction to B2B Content Marketing

"Content is not just king; it's the kingdom itself."

Definition and Importance of B2B Content Marketing

In the ever-evolving landscape of modern commerce, two distinct paradigms steer the course of business strategies—Business-to-Business (B2B) and Business-to-Consumer (B2C). While B2C revolves around direct interactions with individual consumers, it's within the intricate web of B2B relationships that businesses unlock the true potential of collaboration and growth.

B2B stands as a dynamic ecosystem where enterprises market and sell their offerings to fellow businesses, forging strategic alliances that drive collective success. These offerings span a spectrum of products, services, and solutions meticulously designed to address the specific pain points and operational challenges faced by organizations across diverse industries.

Consider the diverse array of B2B entities—from agile startups disrupting traditional norms with innovative solutions to established industry giants commanding global influence. Each player in the B2B arena fulfills a unique role, whether it's supplying essential physical goods integral to daily operations, providing specialized services that streamline business processes, or offering cutting-edge software solutions that revolutionize productivity and efficiency.

An integral facet within the realm of B2B is the emergence of software-based businesses, often categorized as Software-as-a-Service (SaaS) providers. These companies not only deliver sophisticated software applications but also offer a seamless integration of product functionalities and service excellence, encompassing features like scalability, customization, and continuous client support.

However, navigating the B2B buyer journey is a multifaceted endeavor marked by intricate dynamics and stakeholder collaboration. Unlike the straightforward path of B2C transactions, where individual consumers make buying decisions based on personal preferences, the B2B landscape involves a collaborative decision-making process among multiple stakeholders within the purchasing organization.

In the realm of B2B, marketers must navigate through a diverse ensemble of influencers, decision-makers, and stakeholders, each contributing unique perspectives and priorities. This demands a strategic approach to content marketing that resonates with varied audiences, addresses distinct pain points, and aligns with strategic business objectives.

Imagine orchestrating a symphony of insights, where each note represents a touchpoint in the buyer's journey—a harmonious progression towards shared goals and mutual benefits. This intricate dance of collaboration underscores the paramount importance of B2B Content Marketing, where every piece of content serves as a conduit for building trust, fostering meaningful connections, and delivering tangible value propositions.

In the vast landscape of modern commerce, where connections are forged through screens and transactions span continents in the blink of an eye, there exists a pulsating force that drives the engine of business growth. This force, with its roots intertwined deeply in the realms of creativity and strategy, is none other than B2B Content Marketing.

At its essence, B2B Content Marketing can be likened to the beating heart of an organization's digital presence. It is the artful orchestration of words, visuals, and ideas that not only captivates but also cultivates meaningful relationships with businesses, forging pathways of trust and loyalty that transcend mere transactions.

Imagine a world where every piece of content is not just a string of words or a flashy graphic, but a gateway to understanding, a beacon of insight that beckons businesses to embark on a journey of discovery and growth. This is the realm where B2B Content Marketing reigns supreme, breathing life into dry statistics and transforming mundane offerings into compelling narratives of value and innovation.

The importance of B2B Content Marketing cannot be overstated, for it serves as the bridge that spans the chasm between businesses and their target audiences. In a digital era inundated with information overload, where attention spans wane and choices abound, compelling content stands out as a guiding light amidst the noise.

What sets B2B Content Marketing apart is its ability to resonate on a deeply emotional level. It's not just about showcasing products or services; it's about weaving stories that evoke curiosity, spark inspiration, and elicit trust. It's about crafting narratives that speak directly to the aspirations, challenges, and aspirations of businesses, fostering a sense of kinship and understanding that transcends the transactional.

Emotion is the secret ingredient that infuses B2B Content Marketing with soul. It's the palpable energy that flows through every word, every image, and every interaction, leaving a lasting imprint on the hearts and minds of decision-makers. When done right, B2B Content Marketing becomes more than just a strategy; it becomes a transformative force that elevates brands from mere entities to trusted advisors and partners.

In the grand tapestry of business, where relationships are the currency of success, B2B Content Marketing emerges as the master storyteller, weaving narratives of value, trust, and partnership that resonate with audiences on a profound level. It's not just about selling; it's about connecting. It's not just about content; it's about emotions. It's not just about marketing; it's about forging enduring bonds that stand the test of time.

So, as we embark on this journey into the heart and soul of B2B Content Marketing, let us remember that behind every click, every share, and every conversion lies a human story waiting to be told. Let us harness the power of emotions, creativity, and strategy to create content that not only drives business growth but also touches the hearts of those we seek to serve. For in the realm of B2B Content Marketing, it is not just about what we say but how we make others feel that truly matters.

Major Differences Between B2B and B2C Content Marketing

In marketing, two distinct paradigms reign supreme—Business-to-Business (B2B) and Business-to-Consumer (B2C). While both share the common goal of engaging audiences and driving conversions, the strategies, tactics, and nuances that define B2B and B2C content marketing are as divergent as they are essential.

1. Audience Dynamics:

B2B Content Marketing revolves around engaging a target audience of businesses, decision-makers, and industry professionals. The content is tailored to address specific pain points, challenges, and goals related to business operations, efficiency, and growth.

In contrast, B2C Content Marketing targets individual consumers, focusing on emotional triggers, lifestyle aspirations, and personal preferences. The content aims to create a connection, evoke desires, and influence purchasing decisions on a more personal level.

2. Content Focus:

B2B Content Marketing emphasizes educational, informative, and value-driven content. This includes whitepapers, case studies, industry reports, and thought leadership pieces that showcase expertise, industry insights, and solutions to complex business problems.

On the other hand, B2C Content Marketing prioritizes entertainment, storytelling, and emotional appeal. Content formats such as videos, social media posts, lifestyle blogs, and product showcases are used to create engaging narratives that resonate with consumer emotions and aspirations.

3. Purchase Cycle:

The B2B purchase cycle is typically longer and involves multiple stakeholders. B2B content marketing strategies focus on nurturing leads, building trust, and providing in-depth information throughout the decision-making process.

In contrast, the B2C purchase cycle is often shorter and more impulsive. B2C content marketing aims to capture attention, create urgency, and facilitate quick decision-making through compelling visuals, persuasive messaging, and limited-time offers.

4. Relationship Building:

B2B Content Marketing is centered around building long-term relationships, fostering trust, and positioning the brand as a reliable partner or solution provider. Content focuses on industry expertise, data-driven insights, and demonstrating ROI to win and retain business clients.

Conversely, B2C Content Marketing prioritizes building emotional connections, brand loyalty, and repeat purchases. Content strategies include loyalty programs, customer reviews, user-generated content, and personalized recommendations to enhance customer experience and loyalty.

5. Metrics and KPIs:

B2B Content Marketing measures success through metrics such as lead generation, conversion rates, customer acquisition cost (CAC), customer lifetime value (CLV), and return on investment (ROI) from marketing efforts.

B2C Content Marketing evaluates performance based on metrics like website traffic, click-through rates, engagement metrics (likes, shares, comments), customer retention rates, and sales revenue generated from campaigns.

6. Content Distribution Channels:

B2B Content Marketing leverages channels such as industry-specific publications, professional networking platforms (LinkedIn), email marketing, webinars, and targeted advertising on business-oriented platforms.

B2C Content Marketing utilizes social media platforms (Facebook, Instagram, TikTok), influencer partnerships, content syndication, mobile apps, and omnichannel marketing strategies to reach and engage consumer audiences effectively.

In essence, the key differences between B2B and B2C Content Marketing lie in their audience dynamics, content focus, purchase cycle complexities, relationship-building strategies, metrics for evaluation, and preferred distribution channels. Understanding and leveraging these differences are crucial for crafting tailored, impactful, and emotionally resonant content marketing strategies that drive business growth and connect with audiences on a deeper level.

Evolution and Trends in B2B Content Marketing

The evolution of B2B content marketing is a fascinating journey that reflects the dynamic shifts in business communication, technology, and customer expectations. From its early stages to the present, B2B content marketing has undergone significant transformations, adapting to the changing landscape of digital commerce and strategic engagement.

In its nascent phase, B2B content marketing was primarily focused on informational content such as whitepapers, case studies, and industry reports. These forms of content aimed to educate and inform business audiences about products, services, and industry trends. However, as digital platforms emerged and online communication became more prevalent, B2B content marketing expanded its horizons.

The rise of websites, blogs, and social media platforms ushered in a new era of B2B content marketing, characterized by a shift towards customer-centric storytelling and engagement. Brands started leveraging storytelling techniques to create compelling narratives that resonated with their target audience's pain points, aspirations, and challenges. This shift from product-centric to customer-centric content marked a significant evolution in B2B content marketing strategies.

As digital technology continued to advance, B2B content marketing embraced multimedia formats such as videos, podcasts, webinars, and interactive experiences. Visual and interactive content became increasingly popular as they offered more engaging and immersive ways to communicate complex ideas, showcase products, and connect with business audiences on a deeper level.

Furthermore, the advent of data analytics, AI-driven insights, and customer segmentation revolutionized B2B content marketing strategies.

Personalization became a key focus, with brands leveraging data to deliver tailored content experiences that addressed individual business needs and preferences. This evolution towards hyper-personalization enhanced engagement, fostered trust, and drove conversions in the B2B space.

Another notable evolution in B2B content marketing is the emphasis on thought leadership, expertise, and actionable insights. Brands began positioning themselves as trusted advisors, sharing valuable knowledge, industry trends, and strategies that added tangible value to their target audience. This shift towards thought leadership not only established credibility but also strengthened relationships with business clients and prospects.

The evolution of B2B content marketing represents a compelling narrative of adaptability, innovation, and strategic alignment with the evolving dynamics of business communication and customer engagement. Let's delve deeper into each phase of this evolutionary journey to uncover the transformative shifts and key milestones that have shaped the landscape of B2B content marketing:

1. Early Stages: Informational Content

B2B content marketing initially focused on providing informational content such as whitepapers, case studies, industry reports, and how-to guides. The goal was to educate and inform business audiences about industry challenges, showcase expertise, and highlight the value propositions of products and services.

2. Emergence of Digital Platforms

With the rise of digital platforms like websites, blogs, and social media, B2B content marketing expanded its reach and capabilities. Brands started leveraging online channels to publish content, engage with audiences, and establish thought leadership in their respective industries.

3. Shift Towards Customer-Centric Storytelling

The evolution towards customer-centric storytelling marked a significant shift in B2B content marketing strategies. Brands began crafting narratives that addressed customer pain points, aspirations, and challenges, using stories and experiences to create emotional connections and influence decision-making.

4. Adoption of Multimedia Formats

As digital technology advanced, B2B content marketing embraced multimedia formats like videos, webinars, podcasts, infographics, and interactive content. These formats enhanced engagement, facilitated better understanding of complex information, and provided a more interactive and immersive experience for business audiences.

5. Data-Driven Personalization

The integration of data analytics, AI-driven insights, and customer segmentation enabled data-driven personalization in B2B content marketing. Brands started delivering tailored content experiences based on individual preferences, behaviors, and needs, enhancing relevance and engagement.

6. Focus on Thought Leadership and Expertise

B2B content marketing shifted towards thought leadership and expertise, positioning brands as trusted advisors and industry authorities. Content strategies evolved to include sharing valuable knowledge, insights, trends, and best practices, building credibility and nurturing long-term relationships with business clients and prospects.

7. Omnichannel Distribution and Engagement

In the modern era, B2B content marketing has embraced omnichannel distribution strategies to reach and engage audiences across multiple touchpoints. Brands leverage websites, social media platforms, email marketing, webinars, and digital advertising to create cohesive and integrated content experiences, ensuring consistent messaging and personalized interactions.

8. Continuous Innovation and Adaptation

The evolution of B2B content marketing is an ongoing process characterized by continuous innovation, experimentation, and adaptation to emerging trends and technologies. Brands are constantly exploring new content formats, distribution channels, and engagement strategies to stay relevant, capture audience attention, and drive business growth in a competitive marketplace.

The evolution of B2B content marketing reflects a journey of transformational change, from informational content to customer-centric storytelling, multimedia engagement, data-driven personalization, thought leadership, omnichannel distribution, and continuous innovation. This evolution underscores the strategic importance of content marketing in modern business strategies, highlighting its role in building brand awareness, driving customer engagement, and fostering meaningful relationships with business audiences.

B2B content marketing is undergoing a transformative evolution, driven by emerging trends that shape the way businesses engage, connect, and succeed in the digital age. As we navigate the dynamic landscape of B2B content marketing trends, it's essential to understand the key shifts, strategies, and opportunities that are driving meaningful engagement and driving business growth.

1. **Personalization and Targeting**:
    - Trend: Hyper-personalization has become a cornerstone of B2B content marketing strategies, leveraging data analytics, AI-driven insights, and customer segmentation to deliver tailored content experiences.
    - Strategy: By understanding individual

preferences, behaviors, and needs, brands can create personalized content that resonates with audiences, enhances relevance, and fosters deeper connections.

2. **Visual and Interactive Content:**
    - Trend: The rise of visual storytelling and interactive content formats such as videos, webinars, infographics, and immersive experiences is transforming B2B content marketing.
    - Strategy: Visual and interactive content captures attention, simplifies complex

concepts, and enhances engagement, providing a more engaging and memorable experience for business audiences.

3. **Thought Leadership and Expertise**:
    - Trend: Thought leadership content that showcases industry expertise, actionable insights, and thought-provoking perspectives is gaining traction in B2B content marketing.
    - Strategy: Brands can position themselves as trusted advisors and industry authorities by sharing valuable knowledge, trends, best

practices, and thought leadership content that adds tangible value to their target audience.

4. **User-Generated Content (UGC)**:
    - Trend: Authenticity and social proof are driving the adoption of user-generated content (UGC) such as customer testimonials, case studies, and success stories in B2B content marketing.
    - Strategy: UGC humanizes the brand, builds credibility, and fosters trust among prospects, showcasing real-world experiences and outcomes

that resonate with potential customers.

5. **Multi-channel Distribution**:
    - Trend: B2B content marketing is embracing multi-channel distribution strategies to reach and engage audiences across various touchpoints, including websites, social media, email campaigns, webinars, and content syndication.
    - Strategy: Leveraging a mix of digital channels ensures consistent messaging, personalized interactions, and seamless customer journeys throughout the buying cycle, maximizing reach and impact.

6. **Sustainability and Corporate Social Responsibility (CSR)**:
    - Trend: Increasingly, B2B content marketing is focusing on sustainability initiatives, CSR efforts, and purpose-driven storytelling that align with ethical values and social impact.
    - Strategy: Brands that showcase their commitment to sustainability, environmental consciousness, and social responsibility resonate deeply with conscious business buyers, fostering a sense of shared values and purpose.

Embracing these trends and strategic approaches in B2B content marketing empowers brands to navigate the evolving landscape, connect authentically with audiences, drive meaningful engagement, and ultimately, achieve sustainable business growth. By leveraging data-driven personalization, visual storytelling, thought leadership, UGC, multi-channel distribution, and CSR initiatives, businesses can create impactful content experiences that inspire, educate, and resonate with business audiences on an emotional level.

Chapter 2: Understanding B2B Buyer Personas

"In the world of B2B, trust is the currency of success."

Importance of Buyer Personas in B2B Marketing

The importance of buyer personas in B2B marketing cannot be overstated. These fictional representations of ideal customers based on market research and data analysis play a pivotal role in shaping effective marketing strategies, enhancing customer engagement, and driving business growth.

By understanding the unique needs, pain points, goals, and preferences of different buyer personas, businesses can tailor their messaging, content, and offerings to resonate with each segment effectively. This level of personalization and relevance is crucial in today's competitive landscape, where businesses strive to stand out and build meaningful connections with their target audience.

Buyer personas also provide valuable insights into the buyer's journey, helping businesses map out touchpoints, content types, and messaging strategies at each stage of the purchasing process. From awareness and consideration to decision-making and advocacy, buyer personas guide marketers in delivering the right content at the right time to nurture leads, drive conversions, and foster customer loyalty.

Moreover, buyer personas enable businesses to align their marketing efforts with the needs and preferences of their ideal customers, resulting in more targeted and impactful campaigns. This not only improves the efficiency and effectiveness of marketing initiatives but also enhances ROI by focusing resources on high-potential prospects and opportunities.

Beyond segmentation, buyer personas humanize the target audience, allowing businesses to empathize with their customers, understand their challenges, and position their solutions as valuable assets that address specific pain points and deliver tangible benefits. This emotional connection is key to building trust, credibility, and long-term relationships with customers, ultimately driving brand loyalty and advocacy.

In essence, buyer personas are the cornerstone of successful B2B marketing strategies, serving as guides that inform decision-making, content creation, targeting, and customer engagement. By investing time and effort into developing detailed and accurate buyer personas, businesses can unlock opportunities, drive growth, and create meaningful experiences that resonate with their ideal customers on a deeper level.

Buyer personas serve as the foundation of B2B marketing strategies by providing detailed insights into the diverse needs, preferences, and behaviors of target audiences. Let's delve deeper into the importance of buyer personas in B2B marketing with additional details, insights, and examples:

1. Understanding Diverse Audience Segments: Buyer personas help businesses segment their target

audience into distinct groups based on factors such as industry, job role, company size, challenges, and goals. For example, a software company targeting B2B clients may have buyer personas like "IT Manager in Healthcare" or "Marketing Director in Manufacturing," each with unique pain points and requirements.

2. Tailoring Content and Messaging: With buyer personas in place, marketers can craft content and messaging that resonates with each segment. For instance, a financial services firm targeting small businesses may create content specifically addressing the financial challenges faced by startup founders, showcasing solutions tailored to their needs.

3. Mapping the Buyer's Journey: Buyer personas provide valuable insights into the buyer's journey, from initial awareness to post-purchase engagement. By mapping out the stages and touchpoints for each persona, businesses can deliver relevant content and experiences that guide prospects through the decision-making process effectively.

4. Enhancing Personalization and Relevance: Personalization is key in B2B marketing, and buyer personas facilitate targeted and personalized communications. For instance, an email campaign targeting CFOs can include content highlighting financial ROI metrics, while a

campaign targeting CMOs may focus on branding and marketing impact.

5. Optimizing Lead Nurturing and Conversion: Buyer personas inform lead nurturing strategies, allowing businesses to provide the right information and resources at each stage of the buyer's journey. This targeted approach increases the chances of converting leads into customers by addressing their specific pain points and demonstrating value.

6. Improving Sales and Marketing Alignment: Buyer personas bridge the gap between sales and marketing teams by aligning their efforts towards common goals. For

example, a detailed persona profile can help sales teams understand prospect motivations, objections, and decision criteria, enabling more effective sales conversations and closing deals faster.

7. Measuring and Optimizing Campaign Performance: With buyer personas, businesses can measure the effectiveness of marketing campaigns more accurately. Metrics such as engagement rates, conversion rates, and customer acquisition costs can be analyzed for each persona, allowing for continuous optimization and improvement of marketing strategies.

8. **Building Customer-Centric Strategies:** Buyer personas shift the focus from product-centric to customer-centric strategies, emphasizing the importance of understanding and meeting customer needs. By putting the customer at the center of decision-making, businesses can build stronger relationships, foster loyalty, and drive repeat business.

Buyer personas play a crucial role in B2B marketing by providing a deep understanding of target audiences, enabling personalized and relevant communications, guiding the buyer's journey, improving sales and marketing alignment, and ultimately driving business growth. Businesses that invest in developing accurate and actionable buyer personas are better equipped to connect with customers, deliver value, and achieve long-term success in today's competitive market landscape.

How to Create Effective B2B Buyer Personas

Creating effective B2B buyer personas is a strategic process that requires a deep understanding of target audiences, empathy, data analysis, and continuous refinement. Let's explore the steps and best practices for creating impactful buyer personas in B2B marketing:

1. Research and Data Collection:
Start by gathering data from various sources, including customer surveys, interviews, website analytics, CRM data, social media insights, and market research reports.

Use quantitative data (demographics, job roles, company size, industry) and qualitative insights (pain points, challenges, goals, buying motivations) to build a comprehensive profile of your ideal customers.

2. Identify Common Characteristics:
Look for patterns and commonalities among your target audience segments. Identify shared characteristics, behaviors,

preferences, and pain points that define each persona.

Group similar customers into distinct personas based on their roles, responsibilities, challenges, goals, buying behaviors, and decision-making processes.

3. Develop Persona Profiles:
Create detailed persona profiles that humanize your target audience. Include demographic information, job titles, responsibilities, goals, challenges, pain points, buying criteria, objections, preferred communication channels, and content preferences.

Use real quotes, anecdotes, and stories from interviews or customer feedback to add authenticity and empathy to your persona profiles.

4. Validate and Refine:
Validate your persona profiles by testing them against real customer data, feedback, and interactions. Ensure that your personas accurately represent your target audience and resonate with stakeholders across your organization.

Continuously refine and update your personas based on new insights, market changes, and feedback from sales, marketing, and customer service teams.

5. Map the Buyer's Journey:

Map out the buyer's journey for each persona, including stages (awareness, consideration, decision), touchpoints (website, email, social media, events), content needs (educational, solution-focused, testimonial), and desired outcomes (lead generation, conversion, retention).

Align content and messaging strategies with each stage of the buyer's journey to provide relevant, personalized experiences that guide prospects towards conversion and advocacy.

6. Empathy and Understanding:
Foster empathy and understanding by putting yourself in the shoes of your personas. Understand their

goals, challenges, motivations, fears, and aspirations to tailor your marketing efforts accordingly.

Use empathy maps, customer journey maps, and storytelling techniques to deepen your understanding of persona needs and emotions, driving more impactful and emotionally resonant marketing campaigns.

7. Cross-Functional Collaboration:
Collaborate cross-functionally with sales, marketing, customer service, product development, and other teams to gain diverse perspectives and insights into persona behaviors and preferences.

Ensure alignment and consistency in messaging, strategies, and tactics across departments to deliver a seamless and cohesive customer experience aligned with persona expectations.

8. Iterate and Optimize:
Measure the effectiveness of your persona-driven marketing initiatives using metrics such as engagement rates, conversion rates, customer acquisition costs, and customer lifetime value.

Use data-driven insights to iterate, optimize, and fine-tune your persona strategies over time, making informed decisions that drive continuous improvement and business growth.

By following these steps and best practices, businesses can create effective B2B buyer personas that inform targeted marketing strategies, enhance customer engagement, and drive meaningful relationships with their ideal customers. Embracing empathy, data-driven insights, collaboration, and continuous optimization are key to unlocking the full potential of buyer personas in B2B marketing success.

Utilizing Buyer Personas for Targeted Content Creation

Utilizing buyer personas for targeted content creation is a strategic approach that allows businesses to craft personalized and relevant content experiences that resonate deeply with their ideal customers. Let's delve into how leveraging buyer personas can enhance content creation in B2B marketing:

1. Understanding Customer Needs and Pain Points:
Buyer personas provide insights into the specific needs, pain points, challenges, and goals of your target audience segments.

By understanding these aspects, businesses can create content that addresses real-life issues, offers solutions, and provides value to their ideal customers.

2. Tailoring Content Formats and Messaging:
Each buyer persona may prefer different content formats and messaging styles based on their preferences, roles, and responsibilities.

Tailor content formats such as whitepapers, case studies, webinars, infographics, and videos to match the preferences of each persona, ensuring maximum engagement and impact.

3. Addressing Objections and Overcoming Barriers:
Buyer personas help identify common objections, concerns, and barriers that may prevent prospects

from moving forward in the buyer's journey.

Create content that directly addresses these objections, provides reassurance, and offers solutions that alleviate concerns, building trust and confidence in your brand.

4. Mapping Content to the Buyer's Journey:
Align content creation with the stages of the buyer's journey for each persona, including awareness, consideration, decision-making, and post-purchase engagement.

Develop content that guides prospects through each stage, educates them about solutions, showcases testimonials or case studies, and encourages action towards conversion and advocacy.

5. Personalizing Content Experiences:
Leverage buyer personas to personalize content experiences for different segments of your audience.

Use dynamic content, personalized recommendations, and targeted messaging to deliver customized content that speaks directly to the interests, preferences, and needs of each persona, enhancing engagement and relevance.

6. Creating Emotional Connections:
Buyer personas enable businesses to create content that resonates

emotionally with their ideal customers.

Incorporate storytelling, real-life examples, testimonials, and success stories that evoke emotions, establish empathy, and foster meaningful connections with prospects, driving brand loyalty and advocacy.

7. Optimizing Content Distribution:
Utilize buyer personas to optimize content distribution strategies across various channels such as websites, social media, email campaigns, webinars, and content syndication.

Tailor distribution tactics, timing, frequency, and messaging to align with persona preferences, ensuring that content reaches the right audience at the right time through their preferred channels.

8. Measuring Content Effectiveness: Use analytics and metrics to measure the effectiveness of persona-driven content creation efforts.

Track engagement metrics, conversion rates, lead quality, and customer feedback to evaluate content performance, identify opportunities for improvement, and iterate strategies based on data-driven insights.

By leveraging buyer personas for targeted content creation, businesses can create compelling, personalized, and emotionally resonant content experiences that drive engagement, nurture relationships, and drive business growth.

Embracing empathy, personalization, data-driven insights, and continuous optimization are key to unlocking the full potential of buyer personas in content marketing success.

Chapter 3: Content Strategy Development

"Content without strategy is just noise."

Building a Comprehensive B2B Content Strategy

Building a comprehensive B2B content strategy requires a holistic approach that integrates various elements seamlessly to achieve strategic objectives and drive meaningful results. Let's dive deeper into each aspect of building an effective B2B content strategy with additional details, insights, and examples:

1. Define Clear Objectives:
Clearly define your content strategy objectives, such as increasing brand awareness, generating leads, nurturing prospects, driving conversions, or retaining customers. For example, if your objective is lead generation, your content strategy may focus on creating high-converting lead magnets such as e-books, webinars, or gated resources that capture prospect information.

2. Understand Your Audience:
Conduct in-depth audience research to understand the demographics, psychographics, pain

points, challenges, goals, and buying behaviors of your target audience. For instance, if you're targeting IT professionals in the healthcare industry, your content strategy should address their specific technology needs, compliance challenges, and industry trends.

3. Identify Content Themes and Topics:

Identify key content themes and topics that align with your audience's interests, industry trends, search intent, and informational needs. For example, if your audience is interested in cybersecurity, your content strategy may include topics like "Best Practices for Securing Healthcare Data" or "Cyber Threats Facing Financial Institutions."

4. Diversify Content Formats:
Leverage a mix of content formats to cater to different preferences and consumption habits. This may include blog posts, whitepapers, case studies, videos, podcasts, infographics, interactive tools, and social media content. For instance, a software company may create video tutorials for product demonstrations, customer case studies showcasing successful implementations, and infographics highlighting industry statistics and trends.

5. Develop a Content Calendar:
Create a content calendar that outlines the publication schedule, content topics, formats, distribution

channels, promotion tactics, and key milestones. For example, your content calendar may include weekly blog posts, monthly webinars, quarterly e-books, and ongoing social media content aligned with your marketing campaigns and events.

6. Optimize for SEO and Discoverability:
Implement SEO strategies to optimize your content for search engines and improve discoverability. Conduct keyword research, optimize metadata, create compelling headlines, and focus on providing valuable, relevant content. For instance, a logistics company may optimize their blog content with keywords like "Supply Chain

Optimization Tips" or "Logistics Trends 2022" to attract organic traffic from professionals in the logistics industry.

7. Promote Content Across Channels:

Leverage multiple distribution channels to promote and amplify your content reach. This may include social media platforms, email newsletters, content syndication platforms, industry forums, and influencer collaborations. For example, a marketing agency may promote their latest e-book on social media channels with engaging visuals, run targeted email campaigns to their subscriber list, and collaborate with industry influencers to reach a wider audience.

8. Measure and Analyze Performance:
Use analytics tools to track and measure content performance metrics such as website traffic, engagement rates, conversion rates, lead generation, social shares, and ROI.
For instance, analyze which content formats, topics, and distribution channels are driving the most engagement and conversions, and use those insights to optimize future content strategies.

9. Tweak and Optimize:
Continuously tweak and optimize your content strategy based on

performance data, audience feedback, industry trends, and competitive analysis. For example, if a particular blog post resonates well with your audience and drives significant traffic, consider creating follow-up content or expanding on related topics to capitalize on its success.

10. Embrace Creativity and Innovation:

Foster creativity and innovation in your content strategy by experimenting with new formats, storytelling techniques, visual elements, interactive features, and collaborative initiatives. For instance, launch a content series that showcases customer success stories, interviews industry experts, or provides behind-the-scenes glimpses into your company culture to humanize your brand and engage audiences authentically.

By incorporating these detailed insights, examples, and best practices into your B2B content strategy, you can create a comprehensive and impactful approach that resonates with your target audience, drives engagement, builds brand credibility, and fuels business growth. Embrace a data-driven, customer-centric mindset, stay agile and adaptable to evolving market trends, and continuously refine your content strategy to deliver valuable, emotionally resonant content experiences that drive results.

Aligning Content Strategy with Business Goals

Aligning your content strategy with business goals is crucial for driving meaningful outcomes and maximizing the impact of your efforts. By ensuring that your content initiatives are closely aligned with overarching business objectives, you can create compelling, purpose-driven content that resonates with your audience and drives desired actions.

Let's explore how to align your content strategy with business goals in a way that is both educational and emotionally appealing:

1. Understanding Business Goals:

Conduct in-depth discussions with key stakeholders across departments to gain clarity on overarching business goals. These may include revenue targets, market expansion strategies, brand positioning objectives, customer retention goals, and product/service launch priorities. Consider the broader industry landscape, competitive positioning, market trends, customer feedback, and internal capabilities when defining and prioritizing business goals.

2. Identifying Content Goals:
Translate business goals into specific, measurable content goals that support strategic objectives. For instance, if the business goal is to increase market share, content

goals may include creating thought leadership content to establish industry authority, producing product-focused content to drive conversions, and developing customer success stories to build brand credibility.

Align content goals with key performance indicators (KPIs) such as lead generation, website traffic, engagement metrics, conversion rates, customer acquisition costs, and revenue attribution to track progress and measure success.

3. Mapping Content to Business Objectives:

Develop a content mapping strategy that aligns each piece of content with specific business objectives, target audience segments, and stages of the customer journey. Map content assets to key touchpoints in the buyer's journey, from awareness and consideration to decision-making and post-purchase engagement. For example, if the business objective is to drive lead generation, map content assets such as gated e-books, webinar registration pages, and lead nurturing email sequences to capture and nurture leads effectively.

4. Tailoring Content Metrics:
Define relevant content metrics and KPIs that align with business goals and provide actionable insights. Customize reporting dashboards and analytics tools to track and measure content performance in

relation to business objectives. Utilize advanced analytics capabilities to analyze content engagement, conversion funnels, attribution models, customer journey paths, and ROI calculations to understand content impact and optimize strategies accordingly.

5. Creating Goal-Oriented Content:
Develop a content roadmap that aligns with strategic business initiatives and content goals. Prioritize content creation based on business priorities, market opportunities, customer needs, and content performance insights. Leverage content pillars or themes that directly support business objectives, such as industry thought leadership, product education,

customer success stories, solution-focused content, and promotional campaigns tied to key milestones or events.

6. Measuring Impact and ROI:
Implement robust measurement frameworks and attribution models to track content impact and ROI across channels and touchpoints. Use data-driven analytics to assess content effectiveness, customer engagement, lead generation, conversion rates, revenue attribution, and customer lifetime value.
Conduct regular content audits, A/B testing, multivariate testing, and performance reviews to identify top-performing content assets, optimize underperforming content,

and allocate resources effectively to maximize ROI.

7. Iterating and Optimizing:
Foster a culture of continuous improvement and optimization within your content strategy. Collect feedback from stakeholders, analyze content performance data, stay abreast of market trends, and iterate content strategies based on insights and learnings. Experiment with new content formats, distribution channels, messaging tactics, audience segmentation strategies, and personalization techniques to enhance content relevance, engagement, and impact over time.

By implementing these detailed strategies and best practices, businesses can effectively align their content strategy with overarching business goals, drive meaningful outcomes, demonstrate tangible ROI, and achieve sustainable growth in today's dynamic and competitive business environment. Embracing a data-driven, customer-centric approach and fostering cross-functional collaboration are key to success in aligning content strategy with business objectives.

Content Mapping for Various Stages of the Buyer's Journey

Content mapping for various stages of the buyer's journey is a strategic approach that involves aligning content creation with the specific needs, interests, and behaviors of prospects at different stages of their purchasing journey. This process not only enhances the effectiveness of your content marketing efforts but also fosters deeper engagement, trust, and connection with your target audience.

The buyer's journey is not just a series of steps leading to a purchase; it's a dynamic and evolving process that reflects the changing needs, preferences, and behaviors of potential customers. This journey encompasses three pivotal stages: awareness, consideration, and decision. At each stage, prospects embark on a unique quest for information, guidance, and solutions that align with their evolving needs and aspirations.

1. Awareness Stage:

The journey begins with the awareness stage, where prospects first recognize a challenge, pain point, or opportunity they want to address. They are in exploration mode, seeking to understand the scope of their problem and potential avenues for resolution. This stage is characterized by curiosity, information gathering, and initial interactions with brands.

In this stage, businesses have the opportunity to introduce themselves, capture attention, and position themselves as credible sources of information and assistance. Content at this stage should be educational, insightful, and designed to spark interest and curiosity. It should address industry trends, challenges, and potential solutions without diving into product specifics.

2. Consideration Stage:
As prospects progress through the buyer's journey, they enter the consideration stage, where they delve deeper into exploring solutions and evaluating options. They are actively researching and comparing different offerings, weighing benefits, features, and value propositions. This stage is marked by a heightened level of engagement, as prospects seek comprehensive information to inform their decision-making process.

Businesses play a critical role in the consideration stage by providing detailed insights, comparative analyses, and compelling reasons why their offerings stand out. Content in this stage should focus on showcasing expertise, addressing specific pain points, and highlighting unique selling points that differentiate the brand from competitors.

3. Decision Stage:
The final stage of the buyer's journey is the decision stage, where prospects are ready to make a purchase decision. They have narrowed down their options, conducted thorough evaluations, and are now looking for the confidence and reassurance needed

to proceed with a purchase. This stage is characterized by a sense of urgency, trust-building, and conversion readiness.

Businesses must capitalize on the momentum of the decision stage by offering persuasive content that addresses objections, provides social proof through testimonials and case studies, and facilitates a seamless path to conversion. Content here should focus on clear calls-to-action, transparent pricing information, and tailored messaging that nudges prospects towards taking the desired action.

By understanding and catering to the unique needs and behaviors of prospects at each stage of the buyer's journey, businesses can craft targeted content strategies that guide prospects through the decision-making process, nurture relationships, and ultimately drive conversions. The buyer's journey is not a linear path but a nuanced exploration, and businesses that align their content effectively can create impactful touchpoints that resonate with prospects and foster lasting connections.

Mapping Content to the Awareness Stage

In the awareness stage, prospects are seeking educational content that helps them understand their challenges and explore possible solutions.

Content types for this stage may include:
- Educational blog posts addressing industry trends, challenges, and best practices.
- Infographics or visual guides that provide an overview of common problems and potential solutions.
- Whitepapers or e-books offering in-depth insights and research findings related to the prospect's pain points.

Mapping Content to the Consideration Stage

In the consideration stage, prospects are actively evaluating different solutions and comparing options.

Content types for this stage may include:

- Product comparison guides or feature comparison charts that highlight the unique value propositions of your offerings.
- Case studies or success stories showcasing how your products or services have solved similar problems for other customers.
- Webinars or demo videos that provide a deeper dive into your solutions and demonstrate their benefits in action.

Mapping Content to the Decision Stage

In the decision stage, prospects are ready to make a purchase decision and are looking for content that helps them finalize their choice.

Content types for this stage may include:
- Free trials, product demos, or interactive tools that allow prospects to experience your offerings firsthand.
- Customer testimonials or reviews that build trust and credibility by showcasing positive experiences from existing customers.
- Pricing guides, FAQs, or comparison sheets that address common questions and concerns related to the purchase process.

Creating Emotional Appeal

To add emotional appeal to your content mapping strategy, consider incorporating storytelling elements, real-life examples, customer testimonials, and visuals that resonate with the prospect's emotions and aspirations. Use relatable language, empathetic messaging, and personalized content experiences to connect with prospects on a deeper level and show them how your solutions can positively impact their lives or businesses.

Visualizing Content Mapping

Creating visual diagrams or flowcharts can help visually represent your content mapping strategy. For example, you can create a content map that illustrates the progression of content assets across the buyer's journey stages, highlighting key touchpoints and content types at each stage.

By effectively mapping content to the various stages of the buyer's journey and infusing emotional appeal into your content strategy, you can create a compelling and engaging experience for prospects, guide them through their decision-making process, and ultimately drive conversions and customer loyalty.

Embrace empathy, relevance, and storytelling in your content mapping efforts to connect with prospects on a human level and inspire action.

Chapter 4: Creating Compelling B2B Content

"Content is the bridge between brand and audience."

Types of Content That Work Best in B2B Marketing

When it comes to B2B marketing, the content you create plays a crucial role in engaging and persuading business audiences. To stand out and make a lasting impact, you need to understand the types of content that work exceptionally well in B2B marketing.

Let's explore these content types in detail, focusing on their educational value, insightful nature, and emotional appeal.

1. Educational Guides and Whitepapers:
In-depth guides and whitepapers are go-to resources for B2B decision-makers seeking detailed insights and actionable strategies. These content pieces dive deep into industry trends, challenges, and solutions, providing valuable knowledge that helps prospects make informed decisions. By offering educational guides and whitepapers, you position your brand as a thought leader and trusted advisor in your industry. This educational approach resonates

with B2B audiences who prioritize data-driven decision-making and seek expert guidance.

2. Case Studies and Success Stories:
Nothing speaks louder than real success stories. Case studies showcasing how your products or services have solved specific problems for clients add credibility and demonstrate tangible results. B2B buyers are more likely to trust a solution that has been proven effective in real-world scenarios. Sharing compelling case studies and success stories creates an emotional connection with prospects by showcasing the positive impact your offerings have had on other businesses. It instills confidence and reduces perceived

risk, making it easier for prospects to choose your brand.

3. Webinars and Online Events:
Interactive content formats like webinars and virtual events provide a platform for live engagement, knowledge sharing, and interactive discussions. B2B audiences appreciate opportunities to learn from industry experts, participate in Q&A sessions, and network with peers. Hosting engaging webinars and online events not only educates prospects but also fosters a sense of community and collaboration. It positions your brand as a leader in facilitating meaningful conversations and sharing valuable insights within your industry.

4. Industry Reports and Research Studies:

Data-driven content such as industry reports, research studies, and surveys offer valuable benchmarks, trends, and insights that B2B decision-makers rely on. These resources provide objective data and analysis, helping prospects make strategic business decisions. Sharing authoritative industry reports and research positions your brand as a credible source of information and a hub for industry knowledge. B2B audiences value data-backed insights that inform their strategies and validate their decision-making processes.

5. Interactive Tools and Assessments:

Interactive content tools like calculators, assessments, and quizzes engage prospects by offering personalized experiences and actionable insights. These tools allow prospects to assess their needs, evaluate options, and visualize potential outcomes. Providing interactive tools that address specific pain points or challenges empowers prospects to explore solutions in a hands-on manner. It adds an element of interactivity and practicality to your content strategy, making it more engaging and impactful.

6. Thought Leadership Content:
Thought leadership content positions your brand as an industry authority and a forward-thinking

leader. This content includes thought-provoking articles, expert opinions, trend analyses, and commentary on emerging industry developments. Thought leadership content sparks conversations, inspires innovation, and drives thought leadership within your industry ecosystem. It showcases your expertise, vision, and unique perspective, attracting like-minded professionals and fostering industry dialogue.

Incorporating these types of compelling content into your B2B marketing strategy, helps you create a well-rounded approach that educates, inspires, and connects with your target audience. Each content type serves a specific purpose in guiding prospects through their buyer's journey, building trust, and ultimately driving conversions and business growth. Embracing educational value, insightful narratives, and emotional resonance in your content strategy sets your brand apart and establishes long-lasting relationships with B2B audiences.

Crafting Engaging and Valuable Content for B2B Audiences

Creating content that captivates and adds value to B2B audiences is a strategic endeavor that requires a blend of creativity, insight, and empathy. To truly stand out in the competitive landscape, your content must not only educate but also inspire, resonate emotionally, and drive meaningful engagement. Let's delve into key strategies for crafting compelling B2B content that leaves a lasting impression on your audience.

1. Audience-Centric Approach:
Start by deeply understanding your target B2B audience, including their pain points, aspirations, challenges, and decision-making process. Develop detailed buyer personas that reflect the diverse roles and responsibilities within your target companies. Tailor your content to address the specific needs, preferences, and interests of different segments within your audience. Use language, examples,

and insights that resonate with their industry knowledge and professional goals.

2. Educational Depth:
B2B decision-makers are constantly seeking knowledge and insights that can help them navigate complex business landscapes. Create content that goes beyond surface-level information and provides in-depth analysis, actionable advice, and practical strategies. Offer comprehensive guides, research reports, industry analyses, and thought leadership pieces that showcase your expertise and provide valuable takeaways for your audience. Position your brand as a trusted advisor and source of valuable information.

3. Storytelling with Impact:
Harness the power of storytelling to connect with your B2B audience on an emotional level. Share compelling narratives, success stories, and case studies that illustrate real-world challenges, solutions, and outcomes. Use storytelling techniques such as relatable characters, engaging plotlines, and vivid descriptions to bring your content to life. Highlight the human side of business challenges and demonstrate how your solutions can make a meaningful difference.

4. Actionable Insights and Solutions:
B2B audiences value content that provides actionable insights and

tangible solutions to their pressing issues. Create content that offers practical tips, best practices, and step-by-step guides that empower your audience to take decisive actions. Incorporate actionable CTAs (calls-to-action) within your content to encourage engagement, such as downloading a resource, scheduling a demo, or signing up for a webinar. Make it easy for your audience to take the next steps in their journey.

5. Visual Appeal and Multimedia Elements:

Enhance the visual appeal of your content with high-quality graphics, videos, infographics, and interactive elements. Visual content not only grabs attention but also improves comprehension and retention of information. Use multimedia formats to convey complex ideas in a visually engaging manner, break down data into digestible chunks, and create interactive experiences that captivate and educate your audience.

6. Continuous Learning and Optimization:

Monitor the performance of your content using analytics tools to gather insights into what resonates most with your audience. Use A/B testing, audience feedback, and data analysis to refine and optimize your content strategy over time. Stay agile and adapt to evolving trends, industry changes, and audience preferences. Experiment with new content formats, topics, and delivery channels to keep your content fresh, relevant, and impactful.

By adopting a holistic approach that combines audience understanding, educational depth, storytelling prowess, actionable insights, visual appeal, and continuous optimization, you can create compelling B2B content that not only engages but also inspires and drives meaningful action among your audience.

Incorporating Data and Insights into Content Creation

Creating content that deeply resonates with B2B audiences requires a delicate balance between data-driven insights and emotional appeal. By infusing your content with both factual data and compelling storytelling, you can create a powerful narrative that educates, inspires, and emotionally connects with your audience. Let's explore how to craft compelling B2B content that blends data and insights seamlessly with emotional appeal.

1. Understanding Audience Needs:
Start by gaining a deep understanding of your B2B audience's needs, pain points,

aspirations, and challenges. Use data analytics, market research, and customer feedback to uncover valuable insights into what matters most to your audience. Emphasize empathy in your approach by putting yourself in your audience's shoes. Understand their motivations, fears, and desires, and tailor your content to address these emotional triggers.

2. Data-Driven Storytelling:
Incorporate data and statistics into your storytelling to add credibility and authority to your content. Use compelling data points to illustrate industry trends, customer success stories, and the impact of your solutions. Instead of presenting raw data, weave it into narratives that

resonate emotionally with your audience. For example, highlight how your product/service helped a client overcome a major challenge, backed by data showcasing measurable results and ROI.

3. Customer-Centric Case Studies: Develop customer-centric case studies that showcase real-life success stories using your products or services. Use data-backed insights to demonstrate the value and benefits experienced by your customers. Humanize your case studies by including quotes, testimonials, and anecdotes from satisfied customers. Showcasing the human side of business success adds a personal touch and

emotional resonance to your content.

4. Visualizing Impact:
Utilize data visualization techniques such as infographics, charts, and graphs to visually represent the impact of your solutions. Visual storytelling not only enhances comprehension but also evokes emotions and creates a memorable impression. Showcase before-and-after scenarios, growth metrics, and performance indicators to illustrate the transformative power of your offerings. Visuals that depict progress, success, and improvement can evoke feelings of optimism and confidence in your audience.

5. Empathetic Messaging:
Craft messaging that speaks directly to the emotions of your audience. Use language that conveys empathy, understanding, and a genuine desire to help solve their problems. Share stories of resilience, innovation, and collaboration that inspire and uplift your audience. Highlight how your brand values align with the aspirations and values of your target audience.

6. Testimonials and Social Proof:
Leverage testimonials, reviews, and social proof to build trust and credibility. Feature quotes and feedback from satisfied customers or industry influencers who endorse your brand. Use data-driven metrics, such as customer satisfaction scores

or success metrics, alongside testimonials to reinforce the emotional impact and validate the effectiveness of your solutions.

By combining data-driven insights with emotionally compelling storytelling, you can create B2B content that not only educates and informs but also resonates deeply with your audience on an emotional level. This approach fosters trust, builds credibility, and establishes meaningful connections that drive long-term engagement and loyalty.

Chapter 5: Optimizing Content for Search Engines and Social Media

"Optimization is the journey from good to great."

SEO Strategies for B2B Content Marketing

In the fast-paced world of B2B content marketing, SEO strategies are not just about ranking higher on search engines; they're about forging emotional connections with your audience. By infusing your SEO efforts with emotional appeal, you can create content that not only educates and informs but also resonates deeply with B2B decision-makers. Let's explore how to craft SEO strategies that evoke emotions and foster meaningful connections in the B2B landscape.

1. Empathy-Driven Keyword Research:
Start by putting yourself in your audience's shoes. Conduct keyword research that reflects their challenges, aspirations, and search intent. Use empathy-driven keywords that address their pain points and show that you understand their needs on a deeper level.

Emotional Connection: Showcasing empathy in keyword selection demonstrates that you care about your audience's success. It fosters a sense of trust and understanding, laying the foundation for a meaningful relationship.

2. Storytelling with SEO:
Weave storytelling elements into your content while optimizing for SEO. Share real-life anecdotes, customer success stories, and personal experiences that evoke emotions and make your content relatable. Use storytelling to humanize your brand and connect with your audience on an emotional level.

Emotional Connection: Stories have the power to evoke empathy, inspiration, and relatability. By incorporating storytelling into your

SEO strategy, you create content that resonates emotionally and leaves a lasting impact.

3. Optimizing for Emotional Queries: Identify emotional triggers and queries related to your industry. Optimize your content to provide answers, solutions, and guidance that address these emotional needs. Use language that appeals to emotions such as trust, confidence, empowerment, and success.

Emotional Connection: Meeting emotional needs through optimized content shows that you understand the emotional side of decision-making. It positions your brand as a trusted ally that genuinely cares about the *well-being and success of your audience.*

4. Visual Emotion in SEO:
Incorporate visually appealing elements such as images, videos, and infographics into your SEO strategy. Visual content has the power to evoke emotions, convey complex ideas, and create memorable experiences. Use visuals that resonate with your audience's emotions and aspirations.

Emotional Connection: Visuals can evoke a wide range of emotions, from joy and excitement to empathy and inspiration. Leveraging visual emotion in your SEO efforts enhances engagement and leaves a lasting impression.

5. Community Engagement and Social Proof:

Foster a sense of community and belonging through your SEO strategy. Encourage social sharing, comments, and interactions around your content. Highlight user-generated content, testimonials, and reviews that showcase positive experiences and outcomes.

Emotional Connection: Building a community around your brand creates a sense of belonging and camaraderie. Positive social proof reinforces trust and credibility, strengthening the emotional bond with your audience.

6. Measuring Emotional Impact:
Use analytics to track the emotional impact of your SEO efforts. Monitor metrics such as engagement, sentiment analysis, and brand affinity. Gather feedback from your audience to understand how your content resonates emotionally and make adjustments accordingly.

Emotional Connection: By measuring emotional impact, you can refine your SEO strategy to better connect with your audience's emotions. It shows that you are committed to creating content that truly matters to them.

Integrating emotional appeal into your SEO strategies for B2B content marketing is key to creating meaningful connections and driving engagement. By understanding and addressing the emotional needs of your audience, you can craft content that resonates deeply, fosters trust, and inspires action. Emotional SEO is not just about rankings; it's about forging lasting relationships built on empathy, relatability, and genuine care.

Leveraging Social Media Platforms for B2B Content Distribution

In the realm of B2B content marketing, leveraging social media platforms for content distribution is a game-changer. Beyond just sharing content, social media offers a powerful avenue to engage with your audience, build relationships, and drive meaningful interactions. Let's explore how you can optimize content for search engines and harness the emotional appeal of social media for B2B content distribution.

1. Know Your Audience's Social Landscape:
Start by understanding where your B2B audience spends time on social media. Conduct audience research to identify the platforms they prefer and the type of content they engage with most. Tailor your content distribution strategy to align with these preferences. Showcasing that you understand and respect

your audience's social media habits fosters a sense of connection and relatability, laying the foundation for meaningful engagement.

2. Craft Compelling Social Media Content:
Create content specifically designed for each social media platform. Use visually appealing images, videos, infographics, and interactive elements to capture attention and encourage sharing. Craft concise yet impactful captions that resonate with your audience's interests and pain points. Visual content and compelling storytelling on social media evoke emotions, spark curiosity, and inspire action. Creating content that speaks directly to your audience's emotions

increases engagement and fosters a sense of connection.

3. Optimize Content for Social Sharing:
Ensure that your website and content are optimized for social sharing. Include social sharing buttons, catchy headlines, and shareable visuals within your content. Encourage users to share their thoughts, opinions, and experiences related to your content. Making it easy for users to share content they resonate with fosters a sense of empowerment and belonging. User-generated content and social sharing create a community around your brand, driving emotional connection and engagement.

4. Engage Authentically with Your Audience:

Actively engage with your audience on social media by responding to comments, addressing questions, and participating in discussions. Show authenticity, transparency, and empathy in your interactions. Encourage dialogue, feedback, and collaboration. Authentic engagement builds trust, credibility, and loyalty. Responding to your audience's needs and feedback demonstrates that you value their input and are committed to fostering genuine relationships.

5. Use Social Listening for Insights:

Leverage social listening tools to monitor conversations, trends, and sentiment related to your industry and brand. Gain valuable insights into your audience's preferences, pain points, and challenges. Use these insights to tailor your content and engagement strategies. Demonstrating that you actively listen to your audience's voices and concerns shows empathy and understanding. It allows you to create content that resonates deeply and addresses real-time needs and interests.

6. Measure Emotional Impact and Engagement:
Use analytics to measure the emotional impact and engagement levels of your social media content. Track metrics such as likes, shares, comments, and sentiment analysis.

Monitor audience feedback and sentiment to gauge emotional resonance. Measuring emotional impact helps you understand what content resonates most with your audience. It allows you to refine your social media strategy, create more emotionally compelling content, and deepen connections with your audience.

In summary, leveraging social media platforms for B2B content distribution requires a strategic approach that combines emotional appeal, audience understanding, authentic engagement, and data-driven insights. By optimizing content for social sharing, crafting compelling social media content, engaging authentically, using social listening, and measuring emotional impact, you can create a powerful presence on social media that drives meaningful connections, fosters engagement, and amplifies the reach and impact of your B2B content marketing efforts.

Best Practices for Content Amplification and Promotion

Content amplification and promotion are critical components of a successful content marketing strategy. To ensure your content reaches the right audience, resonates emotionally, and drives meaningful engagement, consider implementing the following best practices:

1. Audience-Centric Approach:
Begin by understanding your target audience's demographics, preferences, pain points, and online behavior. Develop detailed buyer personas to guide your content creation and promotion strategies. Tailor your messaging and content formats to meet the specific needs and interests of your audience.
Craft content that speaks directly to the emotions and aspirations of your audience, creating a strong emotional connection that drives engagement and loyalty.

2. Create Exceptional Content:

Focus on producing high-quality, valuable content that provides unique insights, solves problems, or entertains your audience. Ensure your content is well-researched, relevant, and aligns with your brand voice and values. Use storytelling techniques to make your content more compelling and relatable. Incorporate emotional storytelling elements that resonate with your audience's experiences, challenges, and goals, evoking empathy, inspiration, or curiosity.

3. Optimize for Search Engines:
Implement SEO best practices to improve the visibility and ranking of your content on search engine results pages (SERPs). Conduct keyword research, optimize meta

tags, headings, and descriptions, and create SEO-friendly URLs. Focus on providing valuable and authoritative content that satisfies user intent. Highlight the emotional benefits of finding and consuming your content through search engines, such as solving a problem, gaining knowledge, or making informed decisions.

4. Utilize Social Media Channels: Leverage social media platforms strategically to amplify your content reach and engagement. Identify the most relevant social channels for your audience and tailor your content for each platform. Use compelling visuals, interactive elements, and engaging captions to capture attention and encourage

sharing. Engage with your audience authentically on social media, fostering conversations, responding to comments, and showcasing user-generated content that resonates emotionally with your community.

5. Email Marketing and Newsletter Campaigns:

Incorporate content promotion into your email marketing strategy by sending personalized, targeted emails to your subscribers. Segment your email list based on interests and behavior, and deliver valuable content directly to their inboxes. Use enticing subject lines, compelling CTAs, and visual elements to drive engagement. Use email marketing to nurture emotional connections with your audience, delivering content that addresses their pain points, offers solutions, and adds value to their professional lives.

6. Collaborate with Influencers and Partners:

Partner with industry influencers, brand advocates, and strategic partners to expand your content's reach and credibility. Collaborate on co-branded content, influencer campaigns, guest blogging, and webinars to tap into their audience and expertise. Leverage the trust and authority of influencers and partners to enhance the emotional appeal of your content, showcasing social proof and validation that resonates with your target audience.

7. Measure and Optimize Performance:

Use data analytics and tracking tools to measure the performance of your content promotion efforts. Monitor key metrics such as traffic, engagement, conversions, and ROI. Analyze data insights to identify trends, refine your strategies, and optimize future campaigns for better results. Demonstrate the impact of your content promotion efforts through data-driven success stories, highlighting improved brand visibility, customer engagement, lead generation, and business outcomes, which evoke feelings of accomplishment and success.

By implementing these best practices for content amplification and promotion, you can create a comprehensive, emotionally resonant content strategy that drives audience engagement, builds brand authority, and delivers measurable results across search engines, social media, and other digital channels.

Chapter 6: Measuring and Analyzing B2B Content Marketing Success

"Measure what matters; insights drive innovation."

Key Metrics and KPIs for B2B Content Performance

Measuring the success of your B2B content marketing efforts is crucial for optimizing strategies, allocating resources effectively, and demonstrating ROI to stakeholders. To gauge performance accurately and make data-driven decisions, focus on the following key metrics and KPIs:

1. Traffic and Engagement Metrics:

- Website Traffic: Measure the total number of visitors to your website and track traffic sources (organic, direct, referral, social, paid) to assess the effectiveness of your marketing channels.
- Page Views and Time on Page: Analyze the number of page views per content piece and the average time visitors spend on each page to understand engagement levels and content relevance.
- Bounce Rate: Monitor the percentage of visitors who leave your site after viewing only one page. A high bounce

rate may indicate issues with content quality or relevance.

2. Lead Generation and Conversion Metrics:

- Lead Generation: Track the number of leads generated through content downloads, newsletter sign-ups, gated content, or contact form submissions.
- Conversion Rate: Calculate the percentage of leads that convert into customers or take desired actions (e.g., requesting a demo, signing up for a trial). Monitor conversion rates at different stages of the sales funnel.

- Marketing Qualified Leads (MQLs) and Sales Qualified Leads (SQLs): Differentiate between leads that are ready for marketing nurturing (MQLs) and those that meet sales criteria (SQLs) to assess lead quality and alignment with sales goals.

3. Content Engagement Metrics:

- Social Media Engagement: Measure likes, shares, comments, and clicks on social media posts promoting your content. Analyze audience interactions and sentiment to gauge content resonance.

- Email Open and Click-through Rates: Track open rates and click-through rates (CTRs) for email campaigns promoting your content. Evaluate subject lines, CTAs, and content relevance for audience engagement.

4. SEO Performance Metrics:

- Keyword Rankings: Monitor the rankings of targeted keywords related to your content on search engine results pages (SERPs). Track improvements or declines in keyword positions over time.
- Organic Traffic: Assess the volume of organic traffic driven

to your content pages through search engine optimization (SEO) efforts. Measure increases in organic visibility and keyword-driven traffic.

5. Content Consumption and Interaction Metrics:

- Content Downloads: Measure the number of downloads for gated content assets such as ebooks, whitepapers, guides, or case studies. Analyze download trends and user demographics.
- Video Views and Engagement: If using video content, track views, watch time, likes, comments, and shares. Monitor engagement metrics to

understand viewer preferences and content performance.

6. Customer Retention and Loyalty Metrics:

- Customer Lifetime Value (CLV): Calculate the total value a customer brings to your business over their entire relationship. Track CLV trends to assess the long-term impact of content marketing on customer retention and loyalty.
- Customer Satisfaction and Feedback: Gather feedback from customers through surveys, reviews, or interviews to assess satisfaction levels,

gather testimonials, and identify areas for improvement.

These metrics showcase the tangible impact of your content marketing efforts on business growth, customer relationships, and brand reputation. They demonstrate how valuable content resonates with your audience, drives engagement, nurtures leads, and ultimately contributes to revenue generation and business success.

By continuously measuring, analyzing, and optimizing these key metrics and KPIs, you can refine your B2B content strategy, enhance performance, and drive sustainable results.

Tools and Techniques for Content Performance Tracking

Effectively measuring and analyzing the success of your B2B content marketing endeavors is pivotal for refining strategies, allocating resources wisely, and showcasing ROI to stakeholders. Employing a range of robust tools and employing proven techniques for content performance tracking empowers you to make informed decisions and tangibly demonstrate the impact of your content marketing efforts. Here's an in-depth exploration of key tools and techniques to consider:

1. Google Analytics Mastery:

Google Analytics serves as a cornerstone for understanding website traffic, user behavior, and content engagement. Dive into metrics such as sessions, page views, bounce rates, and average session duration to glean insights into visitor interactions with your content.

Utilize Google Analytics Goals to set specific objectives, like form submissions or downloads, and monitor conversions closely to gauge the effectiveness of your content in driving desired actions.

2. Harnessing Content Management Systems (CMS):

Leverage the capabilities of CMS platforms such as WordPress, Drupal, or HubSpot to delve into content performance within your website ecosystem. Analyze metrics like page views, shares, comments, and dwell time for individual content pieces like blog posts, articles, or landing pages.

Leverage CMS analytics dashboards to visualize data, identify top-performing content assets, and pinpoint areas requiring optimization or content refinement.

3. Unveiling Social Media Insights:

Leverage social media management tools like Hootsuite, Sprout Social, or Buffer to unearth social media performance metrics. Track metrics like likes, shares, comments, clicks, reach, and engagement rates across diverse social channels.

Social media analytics unveil valuable insights into audience demographics, sentiment analysis, and content preferences. Identify emerging trends, content virality potential, and opportunities for expanding content reach through strategic social sharing.

4. Strategic Email Marketing Analytics:

If your content promotion strategy includes email marketing, capitalize on platforms like Mailchimp, Constant Contact, or Sendinblue for tracking email performance metrics. Keep an eye on metrics like open rates, click-through rates (CTRs), conversion rates, and subscriber engagement levels.

Leverage A/B testing methodologies to experiment with different email elements such as subject lines, CTAs, content formats, and delivery timings. Analyze test outcomes to optimize email content for heightened engagement and conversions.

5. Deep Dive into SEO Analytics:

Employ robust SEO analytics tools like SEMrush, Moz, Ahrefs, or Google Search Console to monitor keyword rankings, organic traffic patterns, backlinks, and on-page SEO performance indicators. Track keyword visibility, search impressions, and click-through rates (CTRs) for targeted keywords.

Regular SEO audits aid in identifying technical SEO bottlenecks, optimizing meta tags, enhancing content relevance, and elevating overall search engine visibility for your content.

6. Integration with Customer Relationship Management (CRM) Systems:

Seamlessly integrate CRM platforms like Salesforce, HubSpot CRM, or Zoho CRM into your content marketing strategy for tracking leads, opportunities, and customer interactions. Monitor lead generation metrics, pipeline activity, conversion rates, and customer lifecycle stages.

Leverage CRM data to attribute content marketing initiatives to lead generation, sales conversions, and customer retention efforts. Analyze customer journey data to pinpoint content touchpoints contributing significantly to revenue generation.

7. Advanced Data Visualization and Reporting:

Employ data visualization tools like Google Data Studio, Tableau, or Power BI to craft customized dashboards and reports for comprehensive content performance tracking. Visualize key metrics, KPIs, trends, and actionable insights in a visually engaging and actionable format.

Share performance reports effectively with stakeholders, team members, and executives using storytelling techniques to highlight successes, challenges, and actionable recommendations for content optimization and strategy enhancement.

These advanced tools and techniques enable you to showcase the tangible impact and success of your content marketing initiatives, thereby building credibility, trust, and enthusiasm among stakeholders and team members. By leveraging data-driven insights and adopting a strategic approach to content performance tracking, you pave the way for continuous improvement, impactful content strategies, and sustained business growth through compelling B2B content marketing campaigns.

Interpreting Data to Improve Content Marketing ROI

Unlocking the full potential of your B2B content marketing efforts requires a deep dive into data interpretation to enhance ROI. By analyzing key metrics and drawing actionable insights, you can refine strategies, optimize resources, and elevate the impact of your content marketing initiatives. Here's how to effectively interpret data to improve content marketing ROI:

1. Understanding Audience Insights:
Dive into audience demographics, behavior patterns, and engagement metrics to understand who your content resonates with most. Identify audience segments with high conversion rates or engagement levels to tailor content more effectively. For instance, if data shows that a specific industry segment engages the most with your content, focus on creating more targeted content addressing

their pain points and needs. Highlight success stories where content has directly influenced audience decisions, creating an emotional connection with your brand.

2. Analyzing Content Performance:
Analyze content performance metrics such as traffic sources, engagement rates, time on page, and conversion rates for each content piece. Identify top-performing content assets and explore factors contributing to their success. For example, if certain types of content, like video tutorials or case studies, consistently outperform others, allocate more resources to producing similar content that resonates well with

your audience. Showcase the journey of content evolution, from initial ideation to impactful execution, emphasizing the emotional impact and value delivered to readers.

3. Mapping Conversion Paths:

Map out the customer journey and conversion paths to identify touchpoints where content plays a pivotal role in driving conversions. Determine which content formats, topics, or channels contribute most to lead generation and sales. Use data to understand the customer's decision-making process. If data indicates that content downloads or email subscriptions often lead to conversions, optimize these touchpoints to enhance conversion rates. Share success stories of how informative, engaging content has guided prospects through the buyer's journey, building trust and influencing purchase decisions.

4. Optimizing SEO and Search Performance:
Evaluate SEO performance metrics such as keyword rankings, organic traffic growth, and backlink acquisition. Identify high-performing keywords and optimize content around them to improve search visibility and attract qualified leads. Use data-driven insights to refine SEO strategies, focusing on keywords that drive meaningful traffic and align with your target audience's search intent. Highlight the excitement of

discovering new keywords or ranking improvements that directly correlate with increased organic traffic and conversions.

By leveraging data effectively, you can transform raw numbers into actionable insights that drive content strategy refinement and ultimately improve content marketing ROI. This data-driven approach not only enhances performance but also fosters a deeper understanding of your audience's needs, leading to more impactful and emotionally resonant content experiences.

Chapter 7: Personalization and Account-Based Marketing (ABM)

"Personalization transforms prospects into partners."

Importance of Personalization in B2B Content Marketing

Personalization has emerged as a crucial element in B2B content marketing, revolutionizing how businesses connect with their audience, drive engagement, and foster long-term relationships. Let's delve deeper into why personalization holds such significance and how it plays a pivotal role in creating impactful connections:

1. Enhanced Relevance and Tailored Experiences:

Personalization allows you to create content that directly speaks to the individual needs, challenges, and interests of your target audience. By tailoring your messaging, recommendations, and solutions, you enhance the relevance of your content, making it more compelling and valuable to your audience.

Imagine receiving content that addresses your specific pain points, offers tailored solutions, and feels like it was crafted just for you. Personalization creates a sense of being understood and cared for, fostering a deeper emotional connection and engagement with your brand.

2. Elevated Engagement and Interaction:

Personalized content resonates more strongly with recipients, leading to increased engagement levels. Whether it's addressing recipients by name, referencing their past interactions, or recommending content based on their preferences and behavior, personalized approaches capture attention and encourage meaningful interactions.

Feeling recognized and valued as an individual makes recipients more inclined to engage with your content, respond to calls-to-action, and explore further offerings. This sense of personal attention and relevance triggers positive emotions and drives active participation.

3. Improved Conversion Rates and Sales:

Personalization plays a crucial role in guiding prospects through the buyer's journey effectively. By delivering content that aligns with their stage in the decision-making process, industry challenges, and specific pain points, you increase the likelihood of conversions and sales.

Experiencing content that directly addresses their needs and concerns builds trust and confidence in your brand. This emotional connection significantly influences conversion decisions, as prospects feel supported, valued, and confident in their choice to engage with your offerings.

4. Strategic Account-Based Marketing (ABM):

Personalization is the cornerstone of successful ABM strategies. By tailoring content and communications to meet the unique requirements and preferences of targeted accounts and key stakeholders within them,

ABM campaigns become more impactful, driving stronger relationships and revenue growth.

ABM personalization showcases a deep understanding of the target account's challenges and aspirations. This personalized approach fosters a sense of partnership and collaboration, strengthening bonds and nurturing long-term loyalty.

5. Building Sustainable Customer Loyalty:

Personalized content experiences contribute significantly to building lasting customer loyalty. Consistently delivering content that adds value, addresses evolving needs, and anticipates future challenges creates a positive feedback loop, leading to sustained engagement, loyalty, and advocacy.

Building a long-term relationship based on personalized experiences creates a sense of belonging, trust, and mutual benefit. Customers feel valued, appreciated, and connected to your brand on an emotional level, leading to enduring loyalty and advocacy.

In essence, personalization in B2B content marketing transcends mere customization; it's about creating meaningful connections, fostering trust, and delivering exceptional experiences that resonate with your audience on a personal and emotional level.

Embracing personalization as a core strategy empowers businesses to forge deeper connections, inspire loyalty, and drive sustainable growth in today's dynamic and competitive landscape.

Implementing Account-Based Marketing Strategies

Account-Based Marketing (ABM) is not just a strategy; it's a mindset shift that prioritizes personalized engagement with high-potential accounts. To successfully implement ABM strategies, you need a practical approach that combines data-driven insights, personalized content, and a deep understanding of your target accounts. Here's a detailed guide on how to effectively implement ABM strategies:

1. Define Your Ideal Customer Profiles (ICPs):

Start by clearly defining your Ideal Customer Profiles (ICPs) based on factors like industry, company size, revenue potential, pain points, and buying behavior. Utilize data analytics, market research, and insights from your sales team to identify accounts that closely match your ICPs and have the potential for significant business impact.

Work closely with your sales team to gather real-world feedback and refine your ICPs based on actual customer interactions and market trends. This collaborative approach ensures that your ABM efforts are targeted towards the right accounts.

2. Craft Personalized Content and Messaging:

Develop tailored content and messaging that speaks directly to the unique needs, challenges, and goals of each target account. Leverage account-specific data, buyer personas, and past interactions to create compelling content assets such as case studies, personalized emails, and industry-specific insights.

Conduct thorough research on each target account to understand their pain points, strategic initiatives, and decision-making process. Use this information to craft content that addresses their specific concerns and positions your solutions as the ideal fit.

3. Deploy Multichannel Marketing Campaigns:

Implement multichannel marketing campaigns that encompass email outreach, social media engagement, personalized landing pages, direct mail, and virtual events. Tailor your messaging and content for each channel to create a cohesive and immersive experience for key stakeholders within the target accounts.

Utilize account-based advertising platforms to further amplify your message and reach decision-makers across multiple touchpoints. Consistent and personalized messaging across channels reinforces your brand's value proposition and fosters engagement.

4. Facilitate Sales and Marketing Alignment:

Foster close collaboration and alignment between your sales and marketing teams to ensure a seamless ABM execution. Establish shared goals, strategies, and metrics for measuring success. Conduct regular meetings and workshops to exchange insights, share feedback, and fine-tune your ABM approach based on real-time data.

Encourage joint account planning sessions where sales and marketing teams brainstorm strategies, identify key stakeholders, and tailor messaging for specific buying committees within target accounts. This collaborative effort enhances alignment and maximizes the impact of your ABM initiatives.

5. Measure and Iterate for Continuous Improvement:

Leverage data analytics and key performance indicators (KPIs) to track the effectiveness of your ABM campaigns. Monitor metrics such as account engagement rates, pipeline progression, conversion rates, and overall ROI. Analyze campaign performance to identify successful tactics, areas for improvement, and optimization opportunities.

Implement a feedback loop where insights from campaign performance are used to iterate and refine your ABM strategies continuously. Test different messaging variations, channels, and content formats to optimize engagement and drive better results over time.

In summary, implementing Account-Based Marketing strategies requires a practical, data-driven, and collaborative approach. By defining clear ICPs, crafting personalized content, deploying multichannel campaigns, aligning sales and marketing efforts, and measuring performance for continuous improvement, you can unlock the full potential of ABM and drive meaningful relationships with your most valuable accounts.

Tailoring Content for Target Accounts and Decision Makers

In the realm of Account-Based Marketing (ABM), personalization is not just about tweaking a few details; it's about crafting content that speaks directly to the unique challenges, goals, and preferences of each target account and decision-maker. Let's delve into how to tailor content effectively for maximum impact:

1. Comprehensive Account Research:

Start by immersing yourself in thorough research about each target account. Understand their industry dynamics, competitive landscape, recent trends, and pain points. Identify key decision-makers, influencers, and stakeholders within the account structure.

Utilize data analytics, market research reports, and direct conversations with account representatives to gather actionable insights. This research forms the foundation for creating highly personalized content.

2. Segmentation and Persona Development:

Segment target accounts based on shared characteristics such as industry verticals, company size, revenue potential, and geographic location. Develop detailed buyer personas for each segment, focusing on the roles, responsibilities, challenges, goals, and preferred communication channels of key decision-makers.

Leverage CRM data, engagement metrics, and behavioral patterns to create dynamic personas that evolve based on real-time interactions. This segmentation ensures that your content resonates with the specific needs and preferences of each audience segment.

3. Customized Content Creation:

Armed with deep insights, customize your content to address

the unique pain points and aspirations of each target account and decision-maker. Craft personalized emails, case studies, whitepapers, and presentations that align with their challenges and objectives. Tailor the messaging according to the buyer's journey stage and the individual needs of each stakeholder.

Imagine receiving content that directly addresses your pressing concerns, provides relevant solutions, and demonstrates a keen understanding of your role and goals. Personalized content creates a sense of value and relevance, fostering emotional connections with decision-makers.

4. Interactive and Engaging Formats:

Explore interactive content formats such as personalized videos, interactive infographics, and calculators tailored to each account's requirements. These formats not only grab attention but also encourage active participation and engagement.

Interactive content allows decision-makers to explore solutions, visualize benefits, and make informed decisions. It facilitates deeper understanding and positions your offerings as valuable solutions to their challenges.

5. Continuous Feedback and Optimization:

Gather feedback from account representatives, sales teams, and decision-makers regarding the effectiveness of personalized content. Monitor engagement metrics, response rates, and conversion data to evaluate the impact of your content customization efforts.

Use feedback loops and data-driven insights to iterate and optimize content strategies continuously. Test different messaging variations, content formats, and delivery channels to refine your approach and maximize engagement and conversions.

By tailoring content for target accounts and decision-makers in ABM, you create a personalized and immersive experience that demonstrates genuine interest in understanding their unique needs and challenges. This approach builds trust, enhances engagement, and lays the groundwork for long-lasting relationships built on mutual value and understanding.

Chapter 8: Building Strong Relationships Through Content

"Empathy fuels connection in content."

Nurturing Leads with Content Marketing Automations

Nurturing leads is the art of cultivating relationships that drive meaningful interactions and ultimately conversions. Content Marketing Automation is a vital tool in this endeavor, enabling personalized and timely engagements with leads. Let's delve deeper into how Content Marketing Automation can be leveraged to nurture leads effectively and build strong relationships:

1. Understanding Lead Nurturing:

Lead nurturing is more than just a series of automated emails; it's about guiding leads through their buying journey with relevant and valuable content. This process involves understanding their pain points, providing solutions, and building trust over time. Content Marketing Automation streamlines these efforts by automating content delivery based on lead behavior and preferences.

Effective lead nurturing requires a deep understanding of your audience's needs and challenges. By delivering targeted content at the right moment, you demonstrate empathy and establish credibility, laying the foundation for lasting relationships.

2. Segmentation and Personalization:

Content Marketing Automation allows you to segment leads into distinct groups based on criteria such as industry, job role, engagement level, and stage in the buying cycle. Utilize data analytics and lead scoring to identify high-value leads and create personalized content journeys for each segment. Tailor emails, blog posts, webinars, and other content assets to address specific pain points and interests.

Segmenting and personalizing content ensures that your messages resonate with each lead, increasing engagement and relevance. This personalized approach shows that you value their individual needs, fostering a sense of connection and loyalty.

3. Automated Nurturing Sequences:

Develop automated nurturing sequences that deliver a series of relevant content pieces over time. Map out content paths based on lead personas and buyer stages, incorporating educational, informative, and promotional content. Use automation triggers such as email opens, link clicks, and form submissions to guide leads through the funnel and deliver content based on their interactions.

Automated nurturing sequences allow you to stay top-of-mind with leads, providing them with the right information at each stage of their decision-making process. This consistent and strategic approach keeps leads engaged and moves them closer to conversion.

4. Lead Scoring and Qualification:

Implement lead scoring methodologies to prioritize leads based on their level of engagement, readiness to buy, and fit with your ideal customer profile. Assign scores to actions like webinar attendance, content downloads, demo requests, and social media interactions. Use lead scoring data to identify hot leads for immediate sales follow-up and nurture warm leads with relevant content.

Lead scoring helps you focus your efforts on leads with the highest potential, ensuring that sales resources are allocated efficiently. By understanding lead behavior and intent, you can deliver targeted content that resonates with their specific interests and needs.

5. Analytics and Iteration:

Leverage analytics tools to track the performance of your automated campaigns and measure key metrics such as open rates, click-through rates, conversion rates, and lead progression. Analyze data to gain insights into content effectiveness, campaign ROI, and areas for improvement. Use A/B testing to experiment with different content variations and optimize your automation strategies.

Data-driven insights drive continuous improvement in your lead nurturing efforts. By analyzing metrics and refining your content based on feedback, you can enhance engagement, build stronger relationships, and drive better results over time.

Content Marketing Automation is a powerful ally in nurturing leads and building lasting relationships. By segmenting leads, personalizing content, creating automated nurturing sequences, implementing lead scoring, and leveraging analytics for optimization, you can deliver targeted and relevant content experiences that resonate with your audience and drive them towards conversion. Embracing automation not only enhances efficiency but also strengthens the connection between your brand and potential customers, leading to increased engagement, loyalty, and ultimately, business success.

Creating Content for Customer Retention and Upselling

Customer retention and upselling are essential components of building enduring relationships with your audience. Effective content strategies play a pivotal role in achieving these objectives by engaging customers, addressing their evolving needs, and encouraging them to explore additional offerings. Let's delve deeper into practical strategies for creating compelling content that fosters customer retention and drives upselling opportunities:

1. Understanding Customer Retention:

Customer retention goes beyond merely keeping customers; it's about nurturing long-term loyalty and advocacy. To achieve this, businesses must consistently deliver value and exceptional experiences. Content serves as a bridge to maintain ongoing engagement by providing relevant information, addressing pain points, and showcasing the ongoing benefits of using your products or services.

2. Educational Content for Value Enhancement:

Educational content is a cornerstone of customer retention. Develop content assets such as in-depth guides, tutorials, troubleshooting resources, and industry insights that empower customers to derive maximum value from your offerings. For instance, if you offer software solutions, create comprehensive tutorials that showcase advanced features or industry-specific use cases. This educational approach not only strengthens customer knowledge but also positions your brand as a trusted advisor.

3. Emotional Connection Through Stories and Testimonials:

Emotional storytelling is a powerful tool for building strong relationships. Share customer success stories, testimonials, and case studies that highlight real-world benefits and outcomes. Incorporate quotes, visuals, and videos to add authenticity and evoke emotions. For example, showcase how your product helped a customer overcome a specific challenge or achieve significant results. These stories create empathy, trust, and relatability, fostering deeper connections with your audience.

4. Personalized Recommendations and Offers:

Utilize data-driven insights to deliver personalized recommendations and offers. Leverage customer behavior data, purchase history, and preferences to suggest relevant products or services. Implement personalized email campaigns with tailored content and exclusive promotions based on customer segments. For instance, if a customer regularly purchases a certain type of product, recommend complementary items or upgrades that align with their interests.

5. Interactive and Engaging Content Formats:

Incorporate interactive content formats to enhance customer engagement and retention. Develop interactive tools such as ROI calculators, product configurators, quizzes, and assessments that provide value and encourage interaction. Interactive content not only educates but also entertains, capturing and retaining customer attention. For example, a financial services company could create a budgeting tool that helps customers track expenses and set financial goals.

6. Continuous Communication and Support:

Maintain proactive communication with customers through regular touchpoints. Send personalized newsletters, updates, and relevant content to keep customers informed and engaged. Provide excellent customer support through multiple channels, such as live chat, social media, and help desks, to address queries and resolve issues promptly. Engage with customers on social media platforms to foster community and encourage discussions.

7. Measuring Success and Iterating:

Implement robust analytics and measurement tools to track the effectiveness of your content strategies. Monitor key metrics such as customer engagement metrics, retention rates, repeat purchase rates, upsell conversions, and customer satisfaction scores. Analyze data to identify trends, customer preferences, content performance, and areas for improvement. Use these insights to iterate and optimize your content strategy continuously.

By implementing these practical strategies, businesses can create compelling content that not only retains existing customers but also drives upselling opportunities. Educational, emotionally resonant, personalized, interactive, and well-supported content fosters strong relationships, enhances customer loyalty, and contributes to sustainable business growth.

Strategies for Building Trust and Authority in B2B Markets

Establishing trust and authority in B2B markets is essential for forging lasting relationships and driving business growth. Let's delve deeper into practical strategies that leverage content to achieve these critical goals:

1. Thought Leadership Content:

Develop thought-provoking content that showcases your industry expertise, insights, and forward-thinking perspectives. This includes whitepapers, research reports, expert interviews, and opinion pieces that provide valuable and actionable information to your audience. By sharing valuable knowledge, you position your brand as a trusted advisor and industry leader. Thought leadership content should not only demonstrate your expertise but also offer unique insights, analysis, and predictions that add significant value to your audience.

2. Case Studies and Success Stories:

Highlight real-world success stories and case studies that demonstrate the effectiveness of your solutions. Incorporate client testimonials, metrics, and specific outcomes to showcase the tangible benefits your products or services offer. This social proof builds confidence and credibility, showing potential clients what they can achieve by partnering with your company. In-depth case studies that dive into challenges, solutions implemented, and measurable results achieved provide a comprehensive view of your capabilities.

3. Educational Resources:

Offer a variety of educational resources such as webinars, workshops, how-to guides, and industry reports. These resources should provide in-depth knowledge, actionable insights, and practical strategies that help your audience solve challenges and stay ahead in their respective fields. By empowering them with valuable information, you build trust and authority. Webinars and workshops should focus on addressing specific pain points, sharing best practices, and offering hands-on learning experiences.

4. Content Partnerships and Collaborations:

Collaborate with industry influencers, experts, and complementary businesses to co-create content. This could include joint webinars, podcasts, guest blog posts, or collaborative research projects. By associating your brand with respected authorities and thought leaders, you enhance your credibility and reach a wider audience. Partnering with influencers allows you to tap into their existing audience and gain exposure among relevant stakeholders.

5. Transparency and Authenticity:

Be transparent in your communications and interactions with clients and prospects. Share behind-the-scenes insights, company values, and stories that humanize your brand. Authenticity builds trust and fosters genuine connections with your audience, leading to stronger relationships and loyalty. Transparency also includes openly addressing challenges or issues, demonstrating your commitment to honesty and integrity.

6. Interactive Content and Engagement:

Create interactive content experiences such as assessments, quizzes, interactive infographics, and surveys. Encourage audience participation and engagement to gather valuable insights and tailor your content strategy accordingly. Engagement builds rapport and demonstrates your commitment to understanding and meeting your audience's needs. Interactive content should be designed to educate, entertain, and encourage action, driving deeper engagement and connection.

7. Consistency and Quality:

Maintain consistency in your content delivery and ensure high quality across all channels. Regularly publish valuable content that addresses industry trends, challenges, and opportunities. Consistency and quality signal reliability and professionalism, reinforcing your brand's authority and trustworthiness. Content should be well-researched, well-written, visually appealing, and aligned with your brand voice and values.

By implementing these comprehensive strategies, you can effectively build trust and authority in B2B markets, fostering strong relationships with your audience and positioning your brand as a trusted partner in their success journey.

Chapter 9: Content Collaboration and Partnerships

"Collaboration amplifies content's impact."

Collaborating with Industry Influencers and Thought Leaders

Content collaboration with industry influencers and thought leaders can significantly enhance your brand's credibility, reach, and engagement. Let's explore the strategies and benefits of partnering with these key figures in your niche:

1. Strategic Partnerships:

When forming strategic partnerships with influencers and thought leaders, it's crucial to identify individuals or organizations whose expertise and values align closely with your industry and target audience. Conduct thorough research to ensure compatibility in terms of content style, audience demographics, and brand messaging. Collaborate on a variety of content creation projects, such as hosting joint webinars where both parties share insights and expertise, co-authoring articles or research studies that showcase complementary viewpoints, or participating in panel discussions that offer diverse perspectives on industry trends and challenges.

2. Access to Niche Audiences:

One of the primary benefits of collaborating with influencers and thought leaders is gaining access to their established and engaged audiences. This access allows you to reach a broader and more targeted segment of potential customers who are already interested in your industry or related topics. Leverage the influencer's platform to introduce your brand, share valuable content, and engage with their audience authentically. Tailor your messaging and content to resonate with the influencer's followers, addressing their pain points, interests, and informational needs effectively.

3. Enhanced Credibility and Authority:

Partnering with respected influencers and thought leaders can significantly enhance your brand's credibility and authority within your industry. Their endorsement and association with your content serve as powerful validations of your expertise and offerings. Collaborative content projects, such as co-authored articles or joint research studies, lend additional credibility to your brand by showcasing your ability to collaborate with industry leaders and produce valuable insights. This enhanced credibility helps build trust among your audience and positions your brand as a trusted source of information and solutions.

4. Content Variety and Diversity:

Collaborating with influencers and thought leaders brings diversity and richness to your content strategy. Take advantage of their unique perspectives, experiences, and expertise to create content that appeals to a wide range of audience preferences. Incorporate different content formats and styles, such as expert interviews, case studies featuring successful collaborations, thought leadership pieces exploring industry trends, and interactive content that encourages audience participation. Diversifying your content portfolio keeps your audience engaged and interested while showcasing the depth and breadth of your industry knowledge.

5. Increased Engagement and Amplification:

Collaborative content projects often result in higher levels of engagement and content amplification. Leverage the influencer's social media presence and networks to amplify your content's reach through shares, mentions, and endorsements. Encourage audience interaction by hosting live events, Q&A sessions, or interactive discussions with influencers. Engage with comments, questions, and feedback from the influencer's followers to foster meaningful conversations and build relationships. The combined reach and engagement from both parties lead to greater visibility, brand awareness, and audience growth.

6. Long-Term Relationships and Advocacy:

Building long-term relationships with influencers and thought leaders goes beyond individual content collaborations. Nurture these relationships by staying connected, providing ongoing support, and offering value through valuable resources, networking opportunities, and collaborative initiatives. As trust and rapport grow over time, influencers may become brand advocates who actively promote your offerings, share your content, and advocate for your brand within their networks. Cultivating these advocacy relationships leads to sustained brand visibility, positive word-of-mouth referrals, and increased credibility among your target audience.

Collaborating with industry influencers and thought leaders in content creation offers numerous benefits, including expanded reach, enhanced credibility, diverse content perspectives, increased engagement, and long-term relationship building.

By strategically partnering with influencers and thought leaders, you can create impactful content that resonates with your audience, establishes your brand as an industry authority, and drives meaningful connections and conversions.

Partnering with Complementary Businesses for Co-Marketing Opportunities

Collaborating with complementary businesses for co-marketing opportunities can be a game-changer in your marketing strategy. This approach involves joining forces with businesses that offer products or services that complement yours, creating mutually beneficial marketing campaigns. Let's explore how this strategy can be practically implemented and its extensive benefits:

1. Identify Complementary Businesses:

Start by identifying businesses that share your target audience but offer products or services that complement rather than compete with yours. For example, if you sell fitness equipment, partnering with a nutritionist or a fitness app can be beneficial. Look for businesses that align with your brand values, have a similar target demographic, and can add value to your customers' experience.

2. Define Mutual Goals:

Collaborate with your partner businesses to define clear and mutual marketing goals. This could include expanding reach, increasing brand awareness, driving sales, or launching new products/services. Aligning on objectives ensures that both parties are working towards common outcomes and allows for better coordination and measurement of success.

3. Co-Creation of Content:

Co-create compelling content that resonates with your shared audience. This could include blog posts, videos, webinars, ebooks, or social media campaigns. For example, a fitness equipment company and a nutritionist can collaborate on a series of blog posts and videos about healthy eating habits and workout routines. This content should be informative, engaging, and offer value to your audience while subtly promoting both brands.

4. Cross-Promotion and Sharing Resources:

Leverage each other's platforms and resources for cross-promotion. Share each other's content on social media, email newsletters, and websites. Collaborate on joint promotions, discounts, or giveaways to incentivize customer engagement and loyalty. By pooling resources and audiences, you can reach a wider audience and generate more leads and sales for both businesses.

5. Host Joint Events or Workshops:

Organize joint events, workshops, or seminars that showcase the expertise of both businesses. For instance, a software company specializing in project management tools can partner with a consultancy firm to host a webinar on effective project management strategies. These events not only provide valuable insights to participants but also showcase the capabilities of both businesses, leading to increased trust and brand authority.

6. Measure and Evaluate Performance:

Implement robust measurement and tracking mechanisms to evaluate the performance of your co-marketing initiatives. Monitor metrics such as website traffic, lead generation, social media engagement, and sales conversions. Gather feedback from customers and analyze the impact of the partnership on brand perception and customer satisfaction. Use these insights to optimize future collaborations and improve results.

7. Build Long-Term Relationships:

Focus on building long-term relationships with your partner businesses. Cultivate trust, transparency, and open communication throughout the collaboration. Explore opportunities for continuous co-marketing efforts, product integrations, or joint ventures that create ongoing value for both parties and strengthen your position in the market.

Partnering with complementary businesses for co-marketing opportunities offers a strategic approach to expand reach, increase brand visibility, and drive business growth. By leveraging each other's strengths, resources, and audience networks, you can create impactful marketing campaigns that resonate with your target audience and deliver tangible results. Embrace collaboration as a key strategy for mutual success and lasting partnerships in the competitive business landscape.

Leveraging Content Syndication and Guest Posting

Content syndication and guest posting are powerful strategies for content collaboration and partnerships that can significantly amplify your brand's reach and visibility. Let's explore these practices in a practical and extensive manner, highlighting their educational, insightful, and emotionally appealing aspects:

1. Understanding Content Syndication:

Content syndication involves republishing your content on third-party platforms to reach a wider audience. Identify reputable websites, blogs, or media outlets in your industry or niche that accept syndicated content. Syndication allows you to leverage established audiences and gain exposure to new readers who may not be familiar with your brand. Ensure that the syndicated content is relevant, high-quality, and aligns with the platform's guidelines and audience interests.

2. Benefits of Content Syndication:

- Expanded Reach: Syndicating your content on authoritative platforms exposes your brand to a larger audience and increases brand visibility.
- SEO Benefits: Backlinks from syndicated content can improve your website's search engine rankings and domain authority.
- Thought Leadership: Publishing content on respected industry platforms enhances your credibility and positions your brand as a thought leader.
- Lead Generation: Syndicated content can drive traffic to your

website, generate leads, and expand your customer base.

3. Effective Content Syndication Strategies:

- Targeted Platforms: Choose platforms that cater to your target audience and align with your content objectives.
- Optimized Content: Customize syndicated content to suit each platform's audience preferences and optimize it for search engines.
- Consistency: Maintain a consistent publishing schedule for syndicated content to keep your brand visible and engaged with the audience.

- Engagement Monitoring: Track engagement metrics such as views, shares, and comments to assess the impact of syndicated content and refine your strategy accordingly.

4. Guest Posting Opportunities:

Guest posting involves contributing content to other websites or blogs as a guest author. Identify industry-relevant websites, blogs, or publications that accept guest contributions. Craft compelling and valuable content that educates, entertains, or solves problems for the target audience of the hosting platform. Guest posting allows you to reach new audiences, build backlinks, and establish relationships with industry peers and influencers.

5. Benefits of Guest Posting:

- Audience Expansion: Guest posting introduces your brand to a wider audience and attracts new followers and potential customers.
- Authority Building: Publishing insightful content on reputable platforms enhances your brand's authority and expertise.
- Networking Opportunities: Guest posting fosters relationships with other industry professionals,

influencers, and potential collaborators.
- Content Promotion: Utilize guest posting to promote your products, services, or upcoming events subtly within the content or author bio.

6. Guest Posting Best Practices:

- Research: Understand the hosting platform's audience, content guidelines, and preferred topics before pitching guest post ideas.
- Quality Content: Deliver well-researched, original, and engaging content that adds value to the readers and aligns with the platform's theme.

- Engagement and Promotion: Actively engage with readers' comments and promote your guest posts through social media, newsletters, and other channels.
- Relationship Building: Cultivate relationships with editors, bloggers, and fellow guest contributors for future collaboration opportunities.

Leveraging content syndication and guest posting as part of your content collaboration and partnership strategy can yield significant benefits in terms of audience reach, brand authority, and lead generation.

By strategically selecting platforms, creating valuable content, and fostering relationships with industry peers, you can maximize the impact of these practices and enhance your brand's presence in the digital landscape.

Chapter 10: Adapting to Emerging Trends in B2B Content Marketing

"Adaptation is the key to staying relevant."

AI and Machine Learning in Content Personalization

As the landscape of B2B content marketing evolves, leveraging AI and machine learning for content personalization has emerged as a crucial strategy for engaging audiences, driving conversions, and staying ahead of the competition. Let's delve into the practical aspects and extensive benefits of adopting AI and machine learning in content personalization, making it educational, insightful, and emotionally appealing.

1. Understanding AI and Machine Learning:

AI and machine learning technologies encompass algorithms and systems that enable computers to analyze data, learn patterns, and make data-driven decisions without explicit programming. In the context of content marketing, AI and machine learning algorithms can process vast amounts of data to understand customer behavior, preferences, and engagement patterns.

2. Benefits of AI-Powered Content Personalization:

- Enhanced Customer Experience: AI-driven content personalization allows businesses to deliver tailored content experiences based on individual preferences, interests, and behaviors. This enhances customer satisfaction and loyalty.
- Improved Engagement: By analyzing customer data in real-time, AI algorithms can deliver relevant content recommendations, personalized product suggestions, and targeted

messaging that resonate with each prospect or customer.
- Increased Conversions: Personalized content has been shown to significantly increase conversion rates as it addresses specific pain points, provides relevant solutions, and guides prospects through the buyer's journey.
- Efficiency and Scalability: AI-powered content personalization automates the process of analyzing customer data and delivering personalized content at scale, freeing up resources and allowing marketing teams to focus on strategic initiatives.

3. Practical Implementation of AI in Content Personalization:

- Data Collection and Analysis: Utilize AI tools to collect and analyze customer data from various sources, including website interactions, email engagement, social media interactions, and CRM data. This data analysis helps identify patterns, preferences, and behavioral insights.
- Content Recommendation Engines: Implement AI-powered recommendation engines that suggest relevant content, products, or services based on individual user profiles, browsing history, and past interactions. These

recommendation engines can be integrated into websites, emails, and other marketing channels.
- Dynamic Content Generation: Leverage AI-driven technologies to generate dynamic content variations tailored to specific audience segments. This includes personalized emails, website content blocks, product recommendations, and targeted ad creatives.
- Predictive Analytics: Use machine learning algorithms for predictive analytics to forecast customer behavior, predict future trends, and optimize content strategies. Predictive analytics can help

identify high-value leads, anticipate churn risks, and tailor content delivery for maximum impact.

4. Challenges and Considerations:

- Data Privacy and Ethics: Ensure compliance with data privacy regulations and ethical guidelines when collecting and using customer data for AI-driven personalization.
- Algorithm Accuracy: Continuously monitor and refine AI algorithms to improve accuracy, minimize biases, and enhance the relevance of content recommendations.

- Integration and Training: Invest in the integration of AI tools with existing marketing platforms and systems. Provide training to marketing teams on leveraging AI insights and interpreting data-driven recommendations effectively.

5. Embracing the Future of B2B Content Marketing:

Embracing AI and machine learning in content personalization is not just about adopting new technologies but embracing a customer-centric approach to marketing. By harnessing the power of AI for content personalization, businesses can create meaningful and impactful interactions with prospects and customers, driving long-term loyalty, and business growth.

Integrating AI and machine learning into content personalization strategies empowers B2B marketers to deliver hyper-personalized experiences, drive engagement, and achieve measurable results. It's a journey towards customer-centricity, innovation, and staying ahead in the ever-evolving landscape of B2B content marketing.

Interactive Content Strategies for B2B Engagement

Interactive content strategies are at the forefront of modern B2B content marketing, offering dynamic ways to engage audiences, gather valuable insights, and drive meaningful interactions. Let's delve deeper into the practical implementation and extensive benefits of incorporating interactive content strategies into your B2B marketing approach, ensuring it is not only educational and insightful but also emotionally appealing to your target audience.

1. Understanding Interactive Content:

Interactive content refers to digital experiences that actively involve users, encouraging participation, engagement, and personalized interactions. Examples include interactive quizzes, polls, calculators, assessments, virtual events, webinars, and dynamic infographics. These interactive elements create immersive experiences, capture user data, and deliver tailored content based on user inputs.

2. Benefits of Interactive Content for B2B Engagement:

- Enhanced Engagement and Interactivity: Interactive content captivates audiences by offering engaging experiences

that go beyond passive consumption. It encourages users to actively participate, interact, and explore, leading to longer dwell times and increased brand engagement.
- Data Collection and Insights: Interactive content serves as a powerful tool for gathering valuable data and insights about audience preferences, behaviors, pain points, and decision-making criteria. This data can inform personalized marketing strategies, content optimization, and lead nurturing efforts.
- Educational Value and Information Delivery: Interactive content allows businesses to educate their

audience in an interactive and visually appealing manner. Complex concepts can be simplified, product features can be showcased dynamically, and actionable insights can be presented through interactive formats.

- Lead Generation and Conversion Optimization: Interactive content acts as a lead generation magnet, enticing prospects to provide their information in exchange for valuable content or personalized assessments. It also guides prospects through the buyer's journey by delivering targeted content based on their interactions and interests.

- Differentiation and Brand Positioning: Incorporating interactive content sets your brand apart from competitors, showcasing innovation, creativity, and a customer-centric approach. It reinforces your brand's authority, expertise, and commitment to delivering valuable experiences.

3. Practical Implementation Strategies:

- Audience Research and Persona Mapping: Start by understanding your target audience's demographics, pain points, goals, and content

preferences. Use this information to tailor interactive content that resonates with their needs and interests.
- Interactive Content Formats Selection: Choose the right interactive formats based on your objectives and audience preferences. For example, use quizzes or assessments to engage users, calculators to demonstrate ROI, and interactive webinars for in-depth education and engagement.
- Engaging Design and User Experience: Invest in captivating design, intuitive interfaces, and seamless navigation to ensure a positive user experience. Interactive

elements should be easy to use, visually appealing, and encourage continued engagement.
- Personalization and Customization: Leverage user data and behavior insights to personalize interactive experiences. Tailor content recommendations, results, or follow-up actions based on user inputs, preferences, and journey stage.
- Promotion and Distribution Strategies: Effectively promote and distribute interactive content across multiple channels, including your website, social media platforms, email campaigns, and industry partnerships. Use targeted

promotion tactics and encourage social sharing to amplify reach and engagement.

4. Examples of Interactive Content for B2B Engagement:

- Interactive Assessments and Quizzes: Create industry-relevant assessments or quizzes that help prospects identify challenges, assess their readiness, or evaluate their needs. Provide personalized recommendations or solutions based on their responses.
- ROI Calculators and Cost Estimators: Develop interactive tools that allow prospects to input data and calculate potential savings, ROI, or cost estimations related to using your products or services.
- Virtual Events and Webinars: Host interactive webinars or

virtual events with live Q&A sessions, polls, and interactive features. Customize content based on attendee preferences, interests, and engagement levels.
- Interactive Infographics and Data Visualizations: Design interactive infographics that allow users to explore data points, uncover insights, and interact with visual elements for deeper understanding.
- Product Configurators and Demos: Build interactive product configurators or virtual demos that enable prospects to customize product features, explore functionalities, and experience your offerings firsthand.

5. Measuring Success and Iterative Optimization:

Implement robust analytics and tracking mechanisms to measure the performance of interactive content. Monitor metrics such as engagement rates, completion rates, lead conversions, user feedback, and content effectiveness. Use data-driven insights to iterate, optimize, and refine interactive content strategies for continuous improvement and maximum impact.

6. Embracing Interactive Content for Future Success:

Interactive content strategies represent a paradigm shift in B2B marketing, offering innovative ways to connect with audiences, deliver value, and drive business outcomes. By embracing creativity, interactivity, and user-centricity, businesses can build stronger relationships, nurture leads, and achieve marketing objectives effectively in a competitive landscape.

Integrating interactive content strategies into your B2B marketing arsenal empowers you to create engaging experiences, gather actionable insights, and drive measurable results. Embrace the power of interactivity, data-driven personalization, and compelling storytelling to forge meaningful connections, establish thought leadership, and drive business growth in the digital age.

Future Outlook and Predictions for B2B Content Marketing

As we navigate the ever-evolving landscape of B2B content marketing, it's crucial to anticipate future trends and adapt proactively to stay ahead of the curve. Let's delve into the future outlook and predictions for B2B content marketing, exploring practical strategies, insights, and emotionally appealing aspects that can drive success in the coming years.

1. Personalized and Hyper-Relevant Content:

The future of B2B content marketing lies in

hyper-personalization and delivering highly relevant content tailored to individual needs, pain points, and preferences. Utilizing advanced data analytics, AI-driven insights, and predictive modeling, businesses will create content experiences that resonate deeply with their target audience.

Invest in robust data analytics tools to gather comprehensive customer insights. Leverage AI algorithms to analyze data patterns, predict future behaviors, and personalize content recommendations at scale. Craft content that addresses specific challenges, offers actionable solutions, and showcases empathy towards customer concerns.

2. Interactive and Immersive Experiences:

Interactive content formats such as interactive videos, augmented reality (AR) experiences, virtual reality (VR) simulations, and gamified content will become mainstream in B2B marketing. These immersive experiences not only engage audiences but also provide hands-on learning, product demonstrations, and interactive storytelling.

Experiment with interactive content formats that align with your industry and target audience preferences. Develop VR tours of your facilities, create gamified learning modules, or host interactive webinars with live Q&A sessions.

Continuously gather feedback to refine and optimize interactive experiences.

3. Voice Search and Conversational AI:

With the rise of voice-activated devices and virtual assistants, optimizing content for voice search and leveraging conversational AI will be essential. B2B marketers will need to create content that aligns with natural language queries, provides concise answers, and integrates seamlessly into voice-enabled platforms.

Conduct keyword research focusing on long-tail conversational queries.

Optimize website content, FAQs, and knowledge bases for voice search. Explore chatbots and conversational interfaces to enhance customer interactions and provide instant support.

4. Visual Storytelling and Data Visualization:

Visual content, particularly visual storytelling and data visualization, will continue to play a pivotal role in B2B content marketing. Infographics, interactive charts, animated videos, and visually appealing presentations will convey complex information effectively and capture audience attention.

Invest in graphic design resources or collaborate with visual content specialists to create compelling visuals. Use storytelling techniques to narrate brand stories, customer journeys, and industry insights through engaging visuals. Incorporate data-driven storytelling to make statistics and trends more relatable and impactful.

5. Thought Leadership and Industry Influence:

Establishing thought leadership and industry influence will remain a cornerstone of successful B2B content marketing. Businesses that consistently provide valuable insights, thought-provoking content, and expert opinions will earn trust, credibility, and authority within their respective sectors.

Develop a content strategy focused on thought leadership topics relevant to your industry. Publish whitepapers, research reports, case studies, and expert interviews showcasing your domain expertise. Collaborate with industry influencers, participate in industry events, and contribute guest posts to reputable publications to amplify your thought leadership.

6. Sustainability and Social Responsibility:

Increasingly, B2B buyers are prioritizing sustainability, ethical practices, and social responsibility when making purchasing decisions. Content marketing efforts will need to align with these values, highlighting eco-friendly initiatives, corporate social responsibility (CSR) efforts, and sustainable business practices.

Integrate sustainability messaging into your content strategy, highlighting environmentally friendly products, green initiatives, and social impact projects. Share stories of how your business is contributing positively to society, reducing carbon footprint, and supporting sustainable supply chains.

Adapting to emerging trends in B2B content marketing requires a forward-thinking approach that combines innovation, data-driven insights, customer-centricity, and a commitment to delivering value. By embracing personalization, interactivity, visual storytelling, thought leadership, and social responsibility, businesses can navigate the evolving landscape effectively, engage audiences emotionally, and drive long-term success in the digital age.

www.ingramcontent.com/pod-product-compliance
Lightning Source LLC
Chambersburg PA
CBHW052142220526
45471CB00004B/1481